THE HEIDI
CHRONICLES
AND OTHER PLAYS

WENDY WASSERSTEIN

THE HEIDI CHRONICLES

AND OTHER PLAYS

Harcourt Brace Jovanovich, Publishers

SAN DIEGO   NEW YORK   LONDON

HBJ

Printed in the United States of America

Library of Congress Cataloging-in-Publication Data

Wasserstein, Wendy.
The Heidi chronicles and other plays / by Wendy Wasserstein.
p. cm.
ISBN 0-15-139985-9
I. Title
PS3573.A798H4   1990
812'.54—dc20   89-28114

Designed by G. B. D. Smith

First edition
A B C D E

CONTENTS

FOREWORD

Reading the plays of Wendy Wasserstein is quite different from seeing the plays of Wendy Wasserstein. In the theatre, they are consistently funny; the comedy sparkles. Yet when one sits down to read these three plays, one is surprised, almost overwhelmed, by their seriousness.

It seems to me that Wendy's plays are plays of *ideas* that happen to be written as comedies. The three heroines, though vastly different, share an essential sadness, but it is a sadness deflected by humor, because these are witty women and they use their wit to devastating effect.

Reading the plays in chronological order clearly charts the growth of a talented writer. *The Heidi Chronicles* is a far more ambitious work than the two that precede it; it shows a mastery of form and technical expertise that is only hinted at in the earlier plays. The much-discussed women's rap-group scene in *Heidi*, for example, manages to be both an affectionate, satiric look back at an earlier time *and* one of the play's pivotal scenes, in which Heidi becomes a committed feminist. When the scene is played correctly on the stage, the comedy balances the anger, unhappiness, and self-awareness that fuel Heidi's conversion.

Wendy's plays are about many things: friendship, lone-liness, independence, achievement. They manage to be at once shrewdly observed and deeply personal. The voice of the au-thor is heard on every page, and it is a caring, loving voice. That is why so many women and a great many men take these plays to heart. I have seen women storm angrily out of *The Heidi Chronicles* when the curtain falls, while others remain in their seats unable to move because they can't stop crying. I have received letters from men asking me how Wendy knew so much about their lives, and I remember older couples coming out of *Isn't It Romantic* and going up to the author to ask how she could possibly have known, in such detail, about their relationship with their daughter.

I leave scholarly analyses of these wonderful plays to future generations of graduate students. Let me simply say that they are about a generation of women—intelligent, at-tractive, educated, *uncommon* women—who, while attempt-ing to deal with their fears and disappointments, manage to define and redefine who they are. At the end of each play, Holly, Janie, and Heidi come to terms with themselves.

Holly, at the end of *Uncommon Women and Others*, admits to her friends that she has been afraid to see them because she hasn't made any specific choices, she's "in tran-sition." But all is not lost—she has a list of options, a "myriad of openings" for the future. She has emerged from under the raccoon coat she took comfort in earlier in the play. In the last minute of *Isn't It Romantic*, Janie Blumberg finally de-cides to unpack her belongings in the apartment she has been living in for months. From now on she will have to take care of herself. And she celebrates the glory of her life by dancing, as the music swells, the curtain falls, and the voice of her lonely, neurotic friend Cynthia Peterson drones on and on about the men she hopes to meet. And, at the end of *The*

Heidi Chronicles, Heidi sits alone in her empty new apartment rocking her adopted baby as the light floods in from the left. She no longer feels "stranded"; she has made her peace with the sense of betrayal that nearly did her in, and is looking forward to a bright future, if not for her then for her daughter.

Wendy's first play was produced by my theatre, Playwrights Horizons, in 1973. It was called, irony of ironies, *Any Woman Can't*. It seems amazing to me that the insecure, shy young woman of those days, with her mass of brown curls and her infectious high-pitched giggle, has become one of the American theatre's most celebrated and beloved authors. But Wendy, like Heidi, is a serious good person, and her considerable achievements have come about because she is good and because she is serious. Talent is important, to be sure, but what you do with that talent—that is the key.

One last thought: the best thing about reading these plays is that they make the reader look forward to the next ones. Wendy is young, and I believe that this volume will be the first of many. There will be more plays, and even better ones, and Wendy's sharp wit and gentle spirit will entertain and instruct us well into the twenty-first century.

ANDRÉ BISHOP
Playwrights Horizons
November 1989

ACKNOWLEDGMENTS

These plays would not have been in their current form without the contribution of the exceptional actors, designers, stage managers, and producers listed at the beginning of each. I would especially like to thank the respective directors, Steven Robman, Gerald Gutierrez, and Daniel Sullivan, for their craft, vision, love of the theatre, and—most important—sense of humor.

Others who have influenced the lives of these plays include Anne Cattaneo, godmother to all three, Lloyd Richards and The Eugene O'Neill Theatre Center, T. Edward Hambleton of the late and much missed Phoenix Theatre, Howard Stein, and Jac Venza, who brought *Uncommon Women* and *Gracious Living* to public television.

The plays were written, moreover, during generous grants from the Guggenheim Foundation, the National Endowment for the Arts, the Fund for New American Plays, and the British–American Arts Association.

I remain eternally grateful to André Bishop, Paul Daniels, Robert Moss, and the past and future staff at Playwrights Horizons for giving me and over two hundred new American playwrights a home.

WENDY WASSERSTEIN

UNCOMMON WOMEN AND OTHERS

To Abner and Bruce

Uncommon Women and Others was presented by The Phoenix Theatre at the Marymount Manhattan Theatre, in New York City, on November 21, 1977. It was directed by Steven Robman; the scenery and lighting were by James Tilton, and the costumes were by Jennifer von Mayrhauser. The cast, in order of appearance, was as follows:

KATE QUIN	*Jill Eikenberry*
SAMANTHA STEWART	*Ann McDonough*
HOLLY KAPLAN	*Alma Cuervo*
MUFFET DI NICOLA	*Ellen Parker*
RITA ALTABEL	*Swoosie Kurtz*
MRS. PLUMM	*Josephine Nichols*
SUSIE FRIEND	*Cynthia Herman*
CARTER	*Anna Levine*
LEILAH	*Glenn Close*

The play was televised for the PBS Great Performances series in May, 1978. It was directed by Steven Robman and Merrily Mossman. The cast remained the same, except that Leilah was played by Meryl Streep. Phylis Geller and Ann Blumenthal were the associate producers, and Jac Venza was the executive producer.

CHARACTERS

In the present:
KATE QUIN
SAMANTHA STEWART
HOLLY KAPLAN
MUFFET DI NICOLA
RITA ALTABEL

At the college:
MRS. PLUMM
SUSIE FRIEND
CARTER
LEILAH

A restaurant in 1978, and six years earlier
at a college for women

KATE QUIN: in business suit, holding an attaché case that she is quite aware of. The attaché case alternately makes her feel like a successful grown-up, or handcuffed. Perhaps the most handsome of the women, she is composed and has always made a good impression. Like Muffet, she knows the potential of being attractive. Unlike Muffet, she's not sure it's nice, or the right image to let people see. Kate always walks with direction, and that's why it's fun to make her stop and laugh.

SAMANTHA STEWART: a gently attractive woman. If another old adage, "Smith is to bed and Holyoke is to wed," is true, it is women like Samantha who have secured Holyoke's side of the claim. Quiet, tasteful, yet always noticeable at a party. Samantha is like a Shetland cable-knit sweater, a classic. The daughter of the mayor of Naperville, she is a closet wit, or she wouldn't have made the friends she did in college.

HOLLY KAPLAN: hair disheveled, yet well cut. She wears expensive clothes that don't quite match, not because she doesn't know what matches, but because she doesn't want to try too hard. That would be too embarrassing. A relier for many years on the adage "If she lost twenty pounds, she'd be a very pretty girl, and if she worked, she'd do very well," Holly has devised a strong moral code of warmth for those you love and wit for those you're scared of. Holly saw the Radio City Easter Show in second grade and planned to convert.

MUFFET DI NICOLA: an attractive woman, wry and cheerful. She is stylish and attractive to men. Her friends agree that she has charm. Muffet's intelligence is quick, but she never dotes on it. As she approaches thirty, she is reexamining her younger tenets that men were just more interesting than women and life would simply fall into place. Muffet's innate charm, however, never belies her complexity and strength.

RITA ALTABEL: In 1966 Rita won a DAR scholarship to Mount Holyoke. In 1968 she walked through the Yale Cross Campus Library with the Yale Crew Team. Rita had cowbells on her dress. In 1976 she wasn't sure if the CIA had put LSD into all polyester shirts, but she knew it was only safe to wear cotton. She refuses to live *down* to expectations. She shouldn't worry about it. Her imagination would never let her.

MRS. PLUMM: housemother of North Stimson Hall. Mrs. Plumm, like the furniture, is straight-backed but cozy. You can't help but giggle in her presence and grow fonder of her dignity with hindsight.

SUSIE FRIEND: pink Villager sweater, pink Villager skirt, pink knee socks, pink yarn in her hair, and Weejuns, of course. Susie is head of freshmen, coordinator of Father-Daughter Weekend, Spring Weekend, Fall House Parties, the student-faculty committee on library responsibility, and never, unfortunately, gets exhausted.

CARTER: a frail girl in an oversized skirt and shirt that she wore all through prep school. She may seem catatonic, but she has a rich inner life—though it is debatable whether she is a genius or just quiet. Carter is inner-directed.

LEILAH: like Kate, a handsome woman. In fact, she is second to Kate in attractiveness and academically. She is tailored almost to the point of rigidity, but behind her rigidity is genuine kindliness and a strong intellect. Her parents are probably high-powered academics. She is serious and somehow seems distant from her friends. She has not told her parents or her friends any of the fears and anxiety she is beginning to feel. Sometimes Leilah spends a great deal of time alone being admirable.

ACT ONE

Scene 1

MAN'S VOICE: The college produces women who are persons in their own right: Uncommon Women who as individuals have the personal dignity that comes with intelligence, competence, flexibility, maturity, and a sense of responsibility. This can happen without loss of gaiety, charm, or femininity. Through its long history, the college has graduated women who helped to make this a better, happier world. Whether their primary contributions were in the home or the wider community, in advocations or vocations, their role has been constructive. The college makes its continuing contribution to society in the form of graduates whose intellectual quality is high, and whose responsibility to others is exceptional.

As MAN'S VOICE *speaks, lights come up on* KATE QUIN *making final adjustments to a restaurant table.* SAMANTHA STEWART *enters. They embrace and speak softly to each other. As* MAN'S VOICE *fades,* KATE *gets up from the table, and* HOLLY KAPLAN *enters.*

SAMANTHA *laughs:* Holly, it's nice to see you.
HOLLY: You too, Samantha. You cut your hair.

SAMANTHA: Yeah. I didn't want to look like Jean Shrimpton anymore.

HOLLY: Katie. How long are you in town for?

KATE: I don't know. I'm here for a women-and-law conference. Very grown-up, huh? I am now the young spokesperson at all the obligatory boring occasions.

HOLLY: How's Robert?

SAMANTHA: Oh, he's fine. He was just cast in a TV pilot. He plays the male ingenue, and he's worried 'cause his hairline is receding.

KATE: Holly, I forgot to tell you. Rita's coming down from Vermont. She told Samantha she had a six-year itch to see us all again.

SAMANTHA: Muffy wrote me and said that Rita was so fat at her wedding that she couldn't even walk down the aisle. She had to be lowered to the altar by a crane. *Pauses.* I don't believe that.

MUFFET *enters and joins the conversation immediately:* Rita was a rotunda. It was pathetic when the orchestra played . . . *Begins to sing "More."* She must sit in bed and eat bonbons all day.

KATE: Gross me out, Muffet.

ALL: Gross me out?

MUFFET: Holly, pumpkin. *Kisses* HOLLY *and touches her hair.* I like your hair. Kate, did you really have to bring your attaché case to the restaurant? Washington isn't that far away. I wish you got into town more often.

KATE: Muffet, I am a very important person now.

MUFFET: Don't you still sneak trashy novels?

HOLLY: I thought of you, Katie, when Jacqueline Susann died.

SAMANTHA: Did you know she had a buttocks enhancement? Eva Le Gallienne told Robert when he was touring in *Cactus Flower.*

MUFFET: Samantha, only you would call an ass lift a "buttocks enhancement."

KATE: Who's Eva Le Gallienne?

HOLLY: She wasn't our year.

Pause.

MUFFET: Kate, how's Iki?

KATE: Well, he still loves me and Mother still asks about him. But . . .

MUFFET: And what's-his-name, the revolutionary . . .

KATE: He left the bookstore and finished law school. He loves me too. Muffet, this is adolescent. I've become a feminist.

HOLLY: Well, Alice Harwitch dropped out of medical school to form a lesbian rock band.

KATE: Gross me out! Does she sleep with women?

HOLLY: I guess so; they live together.

MUFFET: So what? I've taken a stand on birth-control pills. I won't be manipulated by the pharmaceutical establishment.

HOLLY: Well, you're just not a masochist.

MUFFET: Oh, yes, I am. I'm an insurance-seminar hostess.

HOLLY: Muffy, why don't you go to graduate school?

MUFFET: Holly, not all of our fathers invented velveteen and can afford to send us to three graduate schools. Which master's are you on now: design, literature, or history? I can never keep track.

HOLLY: History.

MUFFET: Holly's embarrassed. You know I didn't mean it. You know you're my best. In fact, the one thing I miss in Hartford is having women friends. *Pauses.* Did you read in the alumnae magazine that Nina Mandelbaum, now a landscape architect, got married twice to the same pediatric pulmonary specialist? They had a small wedding in Mexico and then a big religious ceremony in New York. Why Mexico? Do you think he went to medical school in . . .

ALL: Guadalajara!

HOLLY: My parents got hold of that magazine and offered to fly me to Mexico if I thought he had any friends.

SAMANTHA: Did you know that Ca-Ca Phelps is teaching at Yale?

KATE: Stop!

HOLLY: She was one of those people who was with her horse the day of the Cambodia strike. Her real name is Caroline, right? So why does she still insist on calling herself Ca-Ca? Katie, wasn't Ca-Ca a friend of Leilah's?

KATE: I don't know. I really didn't know Leilah's friends very much. *Pauses briefly.* Do you ever think it's odd that none of us have children? I know we're the uncommon bell curve, but I still think it's odd. I can't decide if I want any.

MUFFET: Don't worry. Nina Mandelbaum will bud for all of us. There's a good genetic pool in pediatric pulmonary specialists. So, where's Rita?

KATE: I don't understand what Rita's doing. She's a smart girl.

MUFFET: So what. We're all smart girls.

HOLLY: It's a sexist society.

KATE: I don't have any trouble.

MUFFET: Kate, you don't know what trouble is. You were born in *Holiday Magazine.*

KATE: Really, what does Rita do all day?

HOLLY: Nothing.

KATE: Gross me out!

RITA *enters. She screams out each girl's name and kisses her. After going around the entire table, she begins again and finally sits down.*

RITA: I just called Timmy.

HOLLY: He loves you.

RITA: No. He waits on me. I told you I always wanted a wife. He gives great head though. Kate, I'm really getting into women's things. I've been reading Doris Lessing, and I think when I get it together I'm going to have a great novel.

MUFFET: Rita, how are you getting it together doing nothing?

RITA: I'm getting into my head.

MUFFET, *to* HOLLY: Or Timmy's, as the case may be.

RITA: Kate, I want to hear more about your law firm. I think we need more women lawyers and gynecologists. I won't go to mine anymore, 'cause it's a man. Besides, I heard he had a twin.

SAMANTHA: Oh, but Rita, you really should get a regular checkup.

RITA: Samantha, what's it like being married to Robert?

SAMANTHA: We're very happy.

RITA: I had to train Timmy. He's going to become my Leonard Woolf. Got a match, Muffet?

SAMANTHA: I was going to join a women's group, but I couldn't decide what to take—macramé, bread-baking, or consciousness rap.

MUFFET *lights her cigarette, then Rita's and Holly's on one match.*

RITA: You know, I saw a Bette Davis movie once, and the third one on the match dies. *Puts her arm around* HOLLY. I didn't upset you, Holly, sweetheart?

HOLLY: No. It was planned on my part. I hate the women's movement. I sent an article to *Ms.* and this Noel Schwartz sent me back a personal note saying I was a heretic to the sisterhood. And I ask you, is Holly Kaplan that different from Noel Schwartz? And she's telling me about the sisterhood!

MUFFET: She has problems.

RITA: That's all right, Holly. When we're forty, we'll be incredible.

HOLLY: Rita, when we were graduating, you predicted by thirty.

Pause. RITA *tosses it off.*

RITA: At least at college they appreciated us.

HOLLY: No they didn't. You were miserable. You hated it.

RITA: Well, at least we appreciated us.

MUFFET: I wish I was back there.

KATE: That says something about the quality of your life.

HOLLY: Kate already is incredible.

KATE: I don't think I appreciated women then, as much as I do now.

RITA: Kate, you just lacked imagination.

KATE: Now Carter, for example, was incredibly bright.

MUFFET: Now Carter, for example, was a catatonic.

Pause.

SAMANTHA: Wanna make an announcement?

KATE: What?

SAMANTHA: I'm going to make an announcement. Like at Mount Holyoke. Now let's all pretend we're at the dining-room table.

They clink glasses.

SAMANTHA: Seniors and anybody who will be here for graduation: We need people to sing on Upper Lake, Commencement Eve. Singers are needed both on shore and in canoes. We will be singing show tunes, and—special attraction—"Love Look Away," from *Flower Drum Song*, and, of course, the alma mater. Questions, call . . .
ALL: Susie Friend! *They clap and laugh.*

HOLLY *stands up, agitated and not laughing.*

MUFFET: Holly, what's wrong?
HOLLY: I can't stand hearing clinking glasses. It always makes me feel that at any moment someone will come out in one of those pastel Modess living rooms and tell me to take my feet off the table, dear.

They all clink glasses.

Scene 2

MRS. PLUMM *enters as soon as the girls finish clinking glasses. She addresses her speech to the audience; it will serve as a transition from present to past. The girls are seated behind her. She has prepared arm movements to go with her recitation, which the girls mimic.*

MRS. PLUMM: I'm so glad I have this opportunity to welcome all you girls to tea this year. I'm Mrs. Plumm, housemother of North Stimson Hall. Take your feet off the table, dear. The tea fund was established by Lucy Valerie

Bingsbee, class of 1906, after whom a Vermont orchid bog was recently dedicated by Governor Hoff as the Lucy Valerie Bingsbee Wildflower Sanctuary. I think you girls will find tea here very comfy. I knew Lucy. I never cared for her much.

I hope you all have a good year. There's a bit of a draft in here. If you have any questions or suggestions, please knock on my door at any time before eight P.M. Although I'm not needed to sign overnight slips anymore, I'm still interested in all my girls.

I thought, before the end of tea, I'd read for you, since I've always enjoyed oral interpretation. My friend Dr. Ada Grudder, class of 1928, organized a theater at the Christian Medical College in Nagpur, India. She begs me to visit, but I don't like long trips, and, anyway, it's so pleasant here, especially in the fall. Mmmmmmmmmmm. The cookies look lovely. What are they? Shortbread?

I'd like to read from the poetry of Emily Dickinson, class of 1850. To those of you who are familiar with this reading, please bear with me. Contrary to rumor, I didn't know Emily. *Laughs to herself.* She never accepted visitors.

The heart is the capital of the mind,
The mind is a single state
   heart and mind together make
A single continent.

One is the population
Numerous enough.
This ecstatic nation
Seek—it is yourself.

Turns to girls at restaurant table. Please take your teacups to the long table at the end of the room when you leave. Why doesn't someone close the window? There's still a draft in here. *Exits.*

Scene 3

A college living room. Six years earlier.

MAN'S VOICE: On November 8, 1837, Miss Lyon's Seminary was a place of high excitement. The building had been completed for the school that was to do for young women what Yale and Harvard were doing for young men. The eighty students who enrolled the first year had the vitality and dedication of pioneers.

The girls in the first scene are joined by LEILAH, *attractive, but intense. In one chair is a very frail blonde girl with alabaster skin:* CARTER. *They are joined also by* SUSIE FRIEND, *in tasteful* Villager *turquoise and an engagement ring. The coffee table is set with teacups, milk and sugar, finger sandwiches, and mayonnaise. Led by* SUSIE FRIEND *the girls stand and sing grace, which is "The Lord Is Good to Me" from the Disney movie* Johnny Appleseed. *The attitude toward this varies.*

CARTER *pulls out her chair.* SUSIE *puts her hand on it.*

SUSIE: Oh, no, wait. You can't sit down till Mrs. Plumm comes.
CARTER: Who's Mrs. Plumm?

SUSIE: She's our housemother.

RITA: She has syphilis.

MRS. PLUMM *enters and sits behind a small tea service.* RITA *waves hello. The girls sit down in unison.* SUSIE *clinks a glass with a spoon. All the girls follow in unison.* CARTER *watches.*

SUSIE *stands up:* Announcement, announcement! There'll be sherry and dinner to honor senior choral members at 1886 House. Also, congratulations to Melissa Weex and Ca-Ca Phelps, new chairmen of the Outing Club and Swan Song Soiree. . . .

Everyone applauds. SUSIE *sits down, takes a finger sandwich.*

SAMANTHA: Susie, would you care for mayonnaise?

SUSIE: I couldn't.

MUFFET: Holly could

SUSIE *bites sandwich:* I love finger sandwiches. I'm Susie Friend. *Turns her head to* CARTER.

MRS. PLUMM: Tea's ready, girls.

The girls pick up cups and form a line in front of MRS. PLUMM. SUSIE *is first, then* KATE, RITA, HOLLY, SAMANTHA.

HOLLY: I'll get it for you, Muffy.

MUFFET *and* CARTER *are left on the couch.* MRS. PLUMM *pours first for* SUSIE.

SUSIE: Thank you, Mrs. Plumm. Mrs. Plumm is my favorite housemother. And Earl Grey. I love Earl Grey.

MRS. PLUMM: Dear, would you care for some brandy?

SUSIE: No, thank you. *Turns to* KATE. Kate, do you want a ride to Cambridge this weekend?

MRS. PLUMM *pours for* KATE.

KATE: No. I'm staying here to work.
MRS. PLUMM: Care for some honey, dear?

KATE *shakes her head.* KATE *and* SUSIE *walk back to the couch and sit.*

SUSIE: Well, if you ever need a ride to Cambridge, I go every weekend. *Turns to* CARTER. I used to date Wharton, but that was before I knew what I wanted. *Laughs at her own charm.*
CARTER: Yes.

MRS. PLUMM *pours tea for* LEILAH.

MRS. PLUMM: Leilah, aren't you going to stay with us for tea?
LEILAH: No. I have more reading to do.

RITA *is in front of* MRS. PLUMM.

RITA: I'd like brandy and honey.
SUSIE, *to* CARTER: I'm a senior. Head of freshmen in North Stimson Hall and a psychology major.

HOLLY *is in front of* MRS. PLUMM.

MRS. PLUMM: Holly, dear, I told you I can't permit you to come to tea in pants. It's not fair to the other girls. I'll let you stay this afternoon. But, dear, let's not see it happen again. I know you can do it; you looked very pretty at Gracious Living once.

SAMANTHA *moves up to* MRS. PLUMM *and* HOLLY. *The girls on the couch turn around to watch.*

SAMANTHA: Holly is very pretty in pink.
HOLLY: I'm sorry, Mrs. Plumm.
MRS. PLUMM: Dear, I just don't want our house to get a reputation.
CARTER: Yes.

All the girls are served and seated. MRS. PLUMM *exits.*

MUFFET: You're not sorry, Holly. You loved every minute of it.
KATE: Holly, I don't see what difference it makes to you. Why torment her? It's just a waste of time.
HOLLY: I don't have a skirt.
MUFFET: Oh, come off it, Holly. Your father invented velveteen.
RITA: I think Holly is very pataphysical.
SUSIE: You know, you girls should really sit at Mrs. Plumm's table more often. I see your group running to the end table after she walks into the room.
CARTER: Yes.

They all look at CARTER.

SUSIE: Well, she's very sweet!
SAMANTHA, *sweetly to* CARTER: She doesn't really have syphilis.
SUSIE: Especially you, Kate. Mrs. Plumm admires you. And

you could make some new friends. I notice your nice friend Leilah never comes to dinner anymore. At least try sitting with Mrs. Plumm at Gracious.

SAMANTHA *smiles at* CARTER: Susie, she doesn't know what Gracious Living is.

SUSIE: Don't call a freshman she. It's alienating. I learned that in psychology.

HOLLY: I think Gracious is a cultural excess. When I get out of here, I'm never going to have dinner by candlelight in the wilderness with thirty-eight girls in hostess gowns. Unless, of course, I train for Amazon guerrilla warfare at the Junior League. Also, I can't stomach the way Mrs. Plumm's neck shakes when she pours the sherry.

The girls all shake their necks.

SUSIE: Holly, have you ever been to Gracious at Smith? Ours is much more homey. I'm glad I didn't go there to college. Smith's much too social.

KATE: Not as much as Vassar. I applied there as a safety school.

SAMANTHA: Well, Vassar's just a cut above Connecticut College.

HOLLY: I thought Conn was a good school.

MUFFET: If you like the Coast Guard.

KATE: Aren't Wellesley and Bryn Mawr the most academic?

SAMANTHA: Well, Bryn Mawr, of course. But Wellesley lacks imagination. They just marry Harvard and MIT.

HOLLY: Hands up! Who here got into Radcliffe?

No hands go up.

MRS. PLUMM *appears briefly:* Hands up! Who wants dessert?

No hands go up.

KATE: Gross me out! It's last night's jelly rolls.
CARTER: Yes.
MUFFET: Don't be embarrassed, Holly. You can take them
   up to your room.

The noise of clinking glasses is heard.

GIRL'S VOICE *announces:* Male long distance. Male LD for
   Susie Friend.

SUSIE *throws her napkin on the table and runs out of the
room singing "The Lord Is Good to Me."*

RITA: Hi, I'm Susie Friend. I love finger sandwiches, Earl Grey,
   and Cambridge. I'm a psychology major, head of freshmen in North Stimson Hall, and I wax my legs. I'd let a
   Harvard man, especially from the business or law school,
   violate my body for three hours; Princeton, for two hours
   and fifty minutes, because you have to take a bus and a
   train to get there; Yale, for two hours and forty-five minutes, because my dad went there and it makes me feel
   guilty; Dartmouth, for two hours and thirty minutes, because it takes them time to warm up; Columbia, I just
   don't know, because of the radical politics and the neighborhood. I learned that in psychology. Now, if I could
   have a Wellesley girl, or Mrs. Plumm, that would be
   different.
KATE: Rita, you're so adolescent.
MUFFET: Remember when Rita made Rorschach tests with
   her menstrual blood to summon back Edvard Munch?

HOLLY: Rita, you couldn't go out with a nice boy from Amherst?

MUFFET: It was her interdepartmental project.

RITA: I thought it was very pataphysical.

CARTER: Yes.

SAMANTHA: But Rita, you're still on the DAR scholarship.

KATE: Uch, Rita, gross me out!

RITA: I never let my economic background deter me.

SAMANTHA: Sometimes I wish I'd never left the Midwest.

MUFFET: Oh, Rita, you've upset her.

RITA *puts her arm around Samantha's chair:* Samantha, pumpkin, why don't you make an announcement? *Puts spoon in Samantha's hand and moves glass toward her.* It'll make you feel better.

SAMANTHA: Rita, I've been here almost four years, and I've never made an announcement.

RITA: Well, it always makes Susie Friend feel better.

SAMANTHA: We don't belong to any committees.

HOLLY: Kate's in Phi Beta Kappa.

MUFFET: Holly, you do it. They'll never expect it from you.

HOLLY, KATE, SAMANTHA, RITA, *and* MUFFET *clink their glasses.* HOLLY *stands up.*

HOLLY: Um. Susie Friend has requested a toast.

HOLLY, KATE, SAMANTHA, *and* MUFFET *immediately stand up with their teacups.* CARTER *stares blankly.*

HOLLY, KATE, SAMANTHA, RITA, *and* MUFFET *sing:*
    Tired of books and boring classes,
    Drop your books, fill up your glasses,
    Drink, the girls who think

Of mixing Greek and Latin
With a cool Manhattan . . .

SUSIE *rushes back to the living room and toasts with her teacup.* MRS. PLUMM *enters, toasts, and sings.*

ALL:
And Amherst has its Heidelberg's
And then there's Mory's down at Yale
And when those Harvard boys
Drink to college joys,
It's dull you must agree,
Adding lemon to your tea.

Smith may have its Ice Tea Hours;
We prefer our whiskey sours.
Drink and never think
About tomorrow tonight.

They toast with their teacups, then take their napkins and begin to exit.

SUSIE: There'll be a rule-book test for all freshmen tonight in the living room after Gracious. Mrs. Plumm has promised to bring sherry.
CARTER: Who's Sherry?

Everyone gives a look at CARTER. *As they leave the living room, each girl folds her napkin and puts it in a box.* CARTER *struggles behind.*

SAMANTHA *watches* CARTER: Susie, she doesn't know where to put her napkin.

SUSIE: Don't call a freshman she. It's alienating. I learned that in psychology. Hi, what's your name?

CARTER: Carter.

SUSIE: Well, Carter, we each have a separate napkin cubby compartment. We take them out before and put them back after each meal. Watch Kate fold her napkin. Your napkin, Carter, is washed and pressed every Wednesday and Sunday in time for Gracious. Now your box is right to the left as you enter the dining room. *Takes Carter's napkin, folds it, and puts it away in the cubbyhole.* And, Carter, if you have any questions or you just want to talk about psychology, knock on my door. It has the Snoopy calendar on it. I got the calendar as a present from Kenny at Harvard. I used to date Wharton, but that was before I knew what I wanted. *Winks at* CARTER. Goodnight. Oh, Carter, I would avoid Rita. I don't know what the DAR was thinking of. *Blows her a kiss and exits.*

CARTER *is left sitting, looking at her napkin.*

Scene 4

MAN'S VOICE: The real problem for many educated women is the difficulty they have in recognizing whether they have been a success. . . . Women will be part-time mothers, part-time workers, part-time cooks, and part-time intellectuals. When scholars point out that even the best cooks have been men, the proper answer is, "But what man has been not only the second-best cook, but the third-best parent, the seventh-best typist, and the tenth-best community leader?" Just like the pot of honey that kept renewing itself, an educated woman's capacity for giving is not exhausted, but stimulated, by demands.

MUFFET *is reading the college catalog.* CARTER, *silent, sits on the floor. Suddenly* MUFFET *throws the catalog down.*

MUFFET: I am so tired. Why doesn't someone just take me away from all this? Did you ever notice how walking into Samantha's room is like walking into a clean sheet? She and Susie Friend celebrate Piglet's birthday. Katie says you're very bright. Did I tell you what happened in Chip Knowles' women's-history class today? Do you know Chip Knowles? He always wears chamois shirts and boat shoes from L. L. Bean. You can never find anything you want in those L. L. Bean catalogs. So I just order a decoy duck every year. It makes me feel Waspy. Chip's wife, Libby, graduated first in her class from Vassar. When I told Chip I was a senior and didn't know what I'd be doing next year, Chip told me that Libby doesn't really spend the day mopping and catching tadpoles with Chip, Jr. She may be mopping with her hands, but with her mind she's reliving the water imagery in the *Faerie Queene.*
 Anyway, I thought women's history would be a gut and it wouldn't look as obvious on my record as Marriage and the Family. As it turns out, this class isn't half bad. We read all the basics; the womb-penis inner-and-outer-space nonsense. *The Feminine Mystique, Sexual Politics,* Mabel Dodge's diary. Chip Knowles says women's history is relevant. Do you think women will lose their relevancy in five years? Like "Car 54, Where Are You?"
 Anyway, after two months of reading about suffra-gettes and courageous choices, this French dish comes into

class dressed in a tight turtleneck and skirt. And you know how for seminar breaks everyone brings in graham crackers? Well, this chick brings in homemade petit fours. And she stands in front of the class and tells us she has not prepared her report on Rosie the Riveter because "you girls are wasting your time. You should do more avec what you have down here—*points to her breasts*—than avec what you have up here"—*points to her head*. And in less than five seconds the entire class is giving her a standing ovation; everyone is applauding. Except Holly and Rita, who grabbed the petit fours, and ran out of the room in protest.

I didn't do anything. I felt so confused. I mean this chick is an obvious imbecile. But I didn't think she was entirely wrong either. I guess the truth is, men are very important to me. Well, not more important than you and Holly and Samantha. Well, not always, pumpkin. Sometimes I know who I am when I feel attractive. Other times it makes me feel very shallow, like I'm not Rosie the Riveter.

I suppose this isn't a very impressive sentiment, but I would really like to meet my prince. Even a few princes. And I wouldn't give up being a person. I'd still remember all the Art History dates. I just don't know why suddenly I'm supposed to know what I want to do.

I guess I should think about sleeping with someone tonight to pass the time. Except it's always creepy in the morning. Rita doesn't think so. But Rita's promiscuous. I'm not promiscuous. I just hate going to bed alone. Maybe sometime you can sleep on my floor. It's funny; you're a freshman, and we're seniors. I'm not even worried about next year. I just have to make sure something happens to me.

SAMANTHA *enters, obviously excited:* Oh, hi, Carter. Muffet, I'm in love.

MUFFET: With whom?

SAMANTHA: Robert Cabe. I met him last night and I thought, this is the one I want. He's handsome and talented, and he's better than me and he'll love me. You'll see. I want to be his audience, and have my picture, behind him, in my long tartan kilt, in the *New York Times* Arts and Leisure section.

MUFFET: That's nice, Samantha. Samantha, how come I haven't met my Heathcliff yet?

SAMANTHA: Oh, Muffy, you wouldn't want *him*. They never settle down. Her soul wandered the moors for years. There's no security in that. You want someone who's good for you.

MUFFET: Maybe. *Pauses.* Actually, I don't mind being alone. I like being strong. Like Rosie the Riveter.

SAMANTHA: I know, Muff. You're just more capable than me. Wanna go for a drive?

MUFFET *starts to leave the room:* Yeah, sure. *Pauses.* Bye-bye, Carter.

SAMANTHA: Bye, Carter.

MUFFET: Oh, Carter, I should be back in about an hour or so, so why don't you come up then and we'll talk some more.

MUFFET *and* SAMANTHA *exit.*

Scene 5

CARTER *is seated alone. Gets up and begins ironically to mime modern dance to* MAN'S VOICE.

MAN'S VOICE: Although the attitude of society toward education for women has changed in the last century and a quarter, the intellectual curiosity, hard work, and spirit of adventure are still characteristic of Mount Holyoke. Mary Lyon, sending her early students out across the plains and seas as teachers and missionaries, said, "Go where no one else will go. Do what no one else will do." Some of her 25,000 "daughters" have blazed new trails, like Frances Perkins, Secretary of Labor under President Roosevelt. Others found adventure near at hand. Emily Dickinson went home. Today thousands of alumnae and students are serving their families and their communities with generosity and imagination, leading lives that enrich those they touch, ready to meet the unknown with steadiness and gaiety.

CARTER *sits down exhausted.*

SUSIE *enters, holding a note.*

SUSIE: Hi, Carter. I have a message from your elf. You see, every freshman has a junior sister and a secret senior elf to help her through. That's right: it's your elf who's been leaving candy in your mail and napkin box, and all the other treats, and she'll fix you up on the weekend, and that's real neat. It's fun to see the girls at tea, and Milk 'n' Crackers too, and try and try to guess which one belongs to you. Don't you love Mrs. Plumm? Fall teas are such fun when she brings apricot brandy. Mmmmmmmmmmmmm, real yum! But Milk 'n' Crackers is neat too. Every night the kitchen help leave out crackers, milk, peanut butter, and sometimes Fluff for you. You

...ld come sometime, Carter. It's a real study break for me from my thesis on Claude Lévi-Strauss.

I'm just a messenger here and I can't say who your elf is. But I think she's found you a male caller, hip hurrah! See you later. *Hands* CARTER *the note and exits.*

CARTER *stares blankly at the envelope. She opens it, and Hershey Kisses fall out. She reads the note.*

CARTER:

> For our Carter,
> No one's smarter.
> Your elf has a surprise
> so open your eyes.
> Kanga and Roo
> have a Yale blue for you.

Looks up.

> A terrific date.
> He can't wait.
> We'll double at the game
> but I won't be to blame
> if he's a little odd
> or a bit of a scrod.

Looks out where SUSIE *has exited.*

> Hair by Thursday must be washed for the trip.
> It wouldn't hurt to give the split ends a snip.
> Tonite's the night it must be done.
> I'm sudsing with Ca-Ca and Jill in number one.

Some Hershey Kisses and best wishes.
Bring a hot-water bottle.
See you at Milk 'n' Crackers.

Lovens,
Your elf

CARTER *puts down letter:* Gross—me—out!

Scene 6

MAN'S VOICE: To profit most fully from the undergraduate curriculum, a student should examine for herself not only the nature of her academic interest, but also her conception of the good life and the kind of community she would like to fashion.

KATE *lies reading on a bed. She throws down the book and picks up another one.*

KATE *reads:* "She remembered the way Melissa Blaine with her perfect cameo face had smiled up at Lance. 'Yes,' she said. 'I'm sure you've had most of the desirable women in the city, but I don't want to be among them.' 'Then, I think it's time I changed your mind,' Lance said. Suddenly Lance's hand slid to the back of her gown. With one strong arm he pinned her to his chest so that, try as she might, she could not push him away. He deftly unfastened the buttons of her gown, as if he had had long practice in performing such actions. 'What are you doing? I'm not one of your strumpets!' "

LEILAH *knocks on the door. Like* KATE, *she is very attractive, but, unlike* KATE, *who is obviously quite confident,* LEILAH *prefers to walk with her head down.*

LEILAH: Kate? You're busy.

KATE: I was just reading *The Genealogy of Morals.*

LEILAH: How was dinner?

KATE: Leilah, I don't understand why you never come. Even Susie Friend has been asking for you.

LEILAH: I came in to get the Nietzsche assignment.

KATE: Leilah, you don't think I'm a good person, do you?

LEILAH: Kate, you're very good.

KATE: Then why don't you ever come in here just to visit, instead of always asking for the assignment? Leilah, we roomed together for three years, and now I never see you anymore. You're angry about last year in Greece, aren't you?

LEILAH: That wasn't your fault.

KATE: I felt bad for you when both Iki and Thomas fell in love with me. Leilah, sometimes I think I should apologize to you, and other times I don't know exactly what I should apologize for. I haven't done anything deliberately to hurt you. I want us to stay friends.

LEILAH: I know.

KATE: What are you going to do next year? I don't know what's going to happen if I don't get into law school.

LEILAH: Kate, you're not supposed to hear until April; this is only November.

KATE: Well, I'm Phi Beta Kappa, but I'm worried about my law‑ boards. *Pauses.* Oh, Lei, pumpkin, don't worry. You'll be Phi Bete by June, in time for graduation. Just think, you could be Muffet, or Samantha, or, God forbid,

Rita. What are they going to do with their lives? At least you and I aren't limited.

LEILAH: Did I tell you I applied to anthropology graduate school?

KATE: Why aren't you continuing in philosophy?

LEILAH: I really like anthropology. I want to go to small towns in Iraq. Look, I've made a list of Mesopotamia jokes.

KATE: Leilah, things aren't going to be better for you in Iraq. You don't have to make yourself exotic. You're a smart, pretty girl. And anyway, if you can't leave your room in South Hadley, how are you going to get along in Iraq?

LEILAH: Just fine. Kate, what's the Nietzsche assignment? I have more reading to do.

KATE: You always have more reading to do.

LEILAH *begins to move away.*

KATE: I'm sorry. Let's talk about something else. Like when we were roommates. Okay? Leilah, what do you know about clitoral orgasms?

LEILAH: Well, my gentleman friend, Mr. Peterson, says they're better than others.

KATE: I wonder if I've had any.

LEILAH: Kate, I'm sure you have. It's a fad.

KATE: Well, I never thought I had a problem.

LEILAH: Why don't you ask Rita?

KATE: Rita's fucked up.

They laugh.

KATE: Leilah, are you leaving philosophy because I'm Phi Bete and you're not? That's stupid. The department likes you as much as me.

LEILAH: Katie, I know you're trying but . . . I don't know. I just want to go away. I don't want to have to think about this place anymore. Kate, do you have the assignment?

KATE: Read the last two chapters in *Genealogy of Morals*. *Pauses*. Look, Leilah, I'm sorry. I really am. But it's not my fault. You're always predisposed against me.

LEILAH: Kate, are you going to Milk 'n' Crackers? I'll see you later.

KATE: Leilah, did you know Holly used to pick up men on the Yale green when she was a sophomore? She had clitoral orgasms. But that was a long time ago.

LEILAH: Maybe that's why she gets on with Rita. They have that in common.

KATE: Leilah, that's nasty.

LEILAH, *strongly:* We all have hidden potential, Kate. *Goes to door*. Bye, Katie.

KATE: I'm going to ask Carter to join us for Milk 'n' Crackers. I think she's very bright. It's been a long time since we've had someone new to talk to in this house—LEILAH *exits*—around three years. KATE, *frustrated, goes back to her book.* " 'I'm sorry,' Lance said after a moment. 'I suppose I shouldn't have done that. But you were asking for it. You wanted it. And you enjoyed every second of it.' "

Scene 7

HOLLY *is filling a diaphragm with Orthocreme.* LEILAH *and* RITA *are walking by, and as soon as they see* HOLLY, *they stop and watch.*

MAN'S VOICE: Am I saying that anatomy is destiny? No, it is not destiny. Providing a setting in which these subtle constraints may be overcome is particularly the mission of a college for women.

RITA: Holly, you've got enough Orthocreme in there to sleep with the entire SS *Constitution.*

HOLLY: The instructions say two teaspoonfuls, so I thought I'd see what it's like with a little extra. I don't want to bud. *Pauses.* Now that I have one of these things, whenever I see a boy with a yarmulke, I think he has a diaphragm on his head. I shouldn't have said that. I'll be struck down by a burning bush.

LEILAH: Who are you going to use this thing with?

HOLLY: I don't know. I got it because it made me feel grown up. I could tell my friends stories about the day I got my diaphragm. Doesn't matter. In fact, I hate being mounted.

RITA: Holly, pumpkin, life doesn't really offer that many pleasures that you can go around avoiding the obvious ones.

HOLLY: What kind of pleasure? There's someone on top of you sweating and pushing and you're lying there pretending this is wonderful. That's not wonderful. That's masochistic.

RITA: But it can be your conquest, pumpkin.

LEILAH: This is distorted. Rita, you are manipulative.

RITA: Leilah, I'm not manipulative. Our entire being is programmed for male approval. Now I, on the other hand, want abandonment. I want to do it with everything: dogs, cats, trees, bushes, ashtrays, children, light bulbs, shoe boxes . . .

LEILAH: Rita, don't you want some attachment? Some love?

RITA: From a cock?

LEILAH: Then why are you with Clark?

RITA: He's a wonderful lover.

LEILAH: Clark's a homosexual.

RITA: He's creative. I've had enough of those macho types. Honestly, after I slept with Jack Hall, he shook my hand and said thank you, and Chip Knowles came like a Pop Tart.

HOLLY: Really. Chip Knowles. I guess Libby was busy with the *Faerie Queene*.

LEILAH: But Rita, wouldn't you want the basis of a relationship to be some mutual understanding or . . .

RITA *cuts her off:* Leilah, you're beautiful. You can.

LEILAH: Rita, you're more beautiful than I am.

RITA *demonstrates with her hand the vertical and horizontal qualities of the buildings and roads:* Listen, Leilah, this entire society is based on cocks. The *New York Times*, Walter Cronkite, all the buildings and roads, the cities, philosophy, government, history, religion, shopping malls—everything I can name is male. When I see things this way, it becomes obvious that it's very easy to feel alienated and alone for the simple reason that I've never been included 'cause I came into the world without a penis. Therefore it is my duty to take advantage. Did I ever tell you about the time I left Johnny Cabot lying there after I'd had an orgasm and he hadn't? It was hilarious. And anyway, Leilah, no one will ever do for me what they'll do for you, or Kate, or even Samantha. So I have to take advantage. In my case, it's a moral imperative. I've got to go. I'm auditioning for Clark. He's directing a production of *Another Part of the Forest*. Forest, trees, logs, pinecones, elks . . . *She demonstrates again as she exits.*

HOLLY: I think she's wrong about the shopping malls. *Pauses.* Sometimes I think we have too much external and too little internal input. It's disturbing having sympathy with everyone's point of view. I guess I better put "thing" away in its shell.

LEILAH: Do you know, the first time I ever really understood about diaphragms or sex was from reading *The Group*. I remember when I was twelve taking it down from my parents' library shelf and rereading the passages about Dottie leaving her diaphragm on Washington Square. It was quite titillating. And my parents didn't mind; they were happy I showed an early interest in Seven Sister schools.

HOLLY: Lei, I want to tell you something, but I was embarrassed to in front of Rita.

LEILAH: How can you be embarrassed in front of Rita? She's so embarrassing.

HOLLY: I called someone in Minneapolis today and hung up. I hung up twice.

LEILAH: Who was it?

HOLLY: A doctor I met with Muffet last summer. I thought I'd visit him over Christmas vacation. That's really why I bought "thing" here. He was very responsive on the phone. He said hello before I hung up.

LEILAH: Maybe you shouldn't see a friend of Muffet's.

HOLLY: Oh, Muffet doesn't know him either. We just met him once at a museum. I could tell he liked me. He smiled a lot at my legs. I'm very attractive from the kneecap to the ankle.

LEILAH: I guess I'm going to stay with my gentleman friend, Mr. Peterson, over vacation. Katie thinks he's boring.

HOLLY: He's not boring. See, I didn't want to talk to Minneapolis, because I was afraid I'd start giggling and be self-effacing and my voice would screech. And then I'd start wishing I was Kate or Rita.

LEILAH: Holly, you can't keep wishing you're someone else. You'll be smothered.

HOLLY: Sometimes I want to clean up my desk and go out and say, "Respect me; I'm a respectable grown-up," and other times I just want to jump into a paper bag and shake and bake myself to death.

SAMANTHA & SUSIE *come through the room with Piglet and a cupcake with a candle:*
> Happy birdle dirdle toodle yoodle doodle,
> Happy birdle dirdle toodle yoodle doodle,
> Happy birdle dirdle, dear Piglet,
> Happy birdle dirdle to you.

SUSIE: Make a wish.

SAMANTHA: Isn't he cute?

They run out giggling. LEILAH *and* HOLLY *watch them.*

LEILAH *turns to* HOLLY: We could shake and bake Piglet.

Scene 8

A Judy Collins record, "Both Sides Now," is heard. HOLLY, SAMANTHA, *and* KATE *are drinking sherry. It is very late.*

SAMANTHA: This was my favorite song in high school. My senior year I sent it to a boy who was hitchhiking cross-country. I printed it on the back of a Vermeer postcard from the Chicago Art Institute. It was the only time I've ever written without capitals or punctuation. I also liked the Dave Clark Five a lot in ninth grade. I thought I could marry one of them, 'cause they were more accessible than the Beatles.

KATE: My best was Leonard Cohen. When I was in high school, I wanted to go down like Suzanne with the garbage and the seaweed. Then I heard he had a thing with Joni Mitchell, and there's only so much wistfulness one can stomach.

SAMANTHA *continues to sing.* RITA *enters, excited and triumphant.*

RITA: I've tasted my menstrual blood.

KATE: Uch, Rita, gross me out.

RITA: Germaine Greer says the test of a truly liberated woman is tasting her menstrual blood.

KATE: Rita, that's drivel.

SAMANTHA: She also says women shouldn't wear underwear.

RITA: Who told you that?

SAMANTHA: Robert.

RITA: Robert, Robert. What does he know about it? I think all men should be forced to menstruate—Robert S. McNamara, Baba Ram-Das, John Glenn—all of them except James Taylor; we'll spare him. But the rest of them should be forced to answer phones on a white Naugahyde receptionist's chair with a cotton lollipop stuck up their crotch.

SAMANTHA: Why spare James Taylor?

HOLLY *looks at her, surprised:* Samantha!

SAMANTHA: Robert says I'm a closet wit. *Giggles.*

RITA: The only problem with menstruation for men is that some sensitive schmuck would write about it for the *Village Voice* and he would become the new expert on women's inner life. Dr. David Reuben, taking time out to menstruate over the July Fourth weekend, has concluded that "women are so much closer to the universe because they menstruate, and therefore they seek out lemon-freshened borax, hair spray, and other womb-related items." *Pauses.* And that's why I think we need to talk about masturbation.

KATE: Rita, gross me out!

HOLLY: Rita, have you ever told the DAR how you spend your time here?

KATE, *slightly interested:* Do you really masturbate?

RITA: I know Susie Friend does. She does it in front of her father's picture from the *New York Times*, when he was made Vice President of American Canco.

SAMANTHA, *politely changing the subject:* Anyone want some corn nuts? My mom just sent them from Naperville. You can't get corn nuts east of the Mississippi.

KATE: I don't think Germaine Greer has thought this out properly. Know what I think the ideal society would be? If all women had communal apartments—not poured-concrete socialist apartments—I mean an estate and everyone worked so child care was rotated, and the men came to visit on the weekends and were nice and charming, bright—all those things—but they left on Mondays.

HOLLY: Katie, that's just what it's like here.

KATE: Well, except my plan doesn't get boring. The men who arrive are Arabian millionaires, poets, lumberjacks. Not corporate lawyers, or MBAs.

HOLLY: Katie, you're a snot rag.

RITA: Kate just grew up in *Holiday Magazine*.

SAMANTHA: I couldn't live in a society like that. I guess I'm not as strong as you, Kate.

RITA: Don't worry, Samantha, pumpkin. You're a closet wit.

HOLLY, *dreamily:* I want to be divorced and living with two children on Central Park West.

KATE: Holly, don't you want to fall in love? You don't have

to get married, but it would be nice to have a passion.

HOLLY: Yes, except if I fall in love, it will be because I think someone is better than me. And if I really thought someone was better than me, I'd give him everything and I'd hate him for my living through him.

KATE: You don't really expect to live through someone else, do you?

HOLLY: I think I'd like to very much.

KATE: Piffle, Holly. You're too diffuse. You need to concentrate your efforts.

RITA: Want to play a game?

KATE: Rita, it's too late in the night for tampon bobbing.

RITA: This is a nice game for nice girls. *Gathers the girls together.* Let's each take a turn and say, if we could marry any one of us, who it would be.

SAMANTHA: I'm already pinned.

RITA: That doesn't count. You can only select from our own uncommon pool. Holly, stop edging under the bed. *Pauses.* I'd marry Samantha, 'cause she'd make the best wife, and in a matrimonial situation I could admire her the longest.

SAMANTHA: Would you really marry me?

RITA: Samantha, you're the perfect woman.

SAMANTHA: Rita, now I feel really bad 'cause I wouldn't have picked you, and it would have been nice if everything worked out. This is very difficult, 'cause it would be interesting to live with Rita, and Kate probably has the best future.

HOLLY: How 'bout Susie Friend?

SAMANTHA: You don't marry a girl like that. Too many committee meetings. She'd never be home. Holly, you're sweet and funny, but I couldn't support you, and there would be a problem at the club. I guess I would marry Muffet, 'cause she could get on with the outside world, and Piglet wouldn't drive her crazy. Also, Muffet's glamorous, but she doesn't scare me.

HOLLY: I guess I would be most comfortable being married to Leilah or Rita. I'd never feel that I have to impress them. But when you get right down to it, I'd want to marry Katie. I would consider living through your accomplishments, Katie, and besides, I'm sure if we got married my parents would approve, and one of us would get our picture in the Sunday *Times*.

They laugh.

SAMANTHA: How about you, Kate? Who would you marry?

KATE: I don't know.

HOLLY: You don't have to marry me, Katie. I understand. Maybe you have to settle your career first.

KATE: I guess I never thought about marrying any of you.

RITA: Kate, for a smart woman, you have a stunted imagination.

KATE: Well, if I married one of us, I would probably have to be the main income source. That's excluding the possibility of trust funds. So if I was supporting someone, I guess I would want to marry Carter.

HOLLY: Carter! Gross me out! I'm sorry. That wasn't very nice. I'm sure you'll be very happy together.

KATE: Carter is very bright. And if I'm going to be a boring lawyer, then I'd want to be married to someone who would stay home and have an imagination. Anyway, Carter would *need* me. Holly, I would consider you, because you're such a good person. But then, that would make me feel a little chilly.

RITA: I think we should celebrate.

SAMANTHA: What?

RITA: That none of our marriage proposals has been reciprocated.

SAMANTHA: We don't know. Maybe Muffy would want to marry me.

HOLLY: No. I think if we marry, we'll have to marry outside of each other. Probably men.

RITA: Muffy's out with Pink Pants. She knows she has to marry a man.

SAMANTHA: I know a great song we could celebrate with and dance to. *Goes to record player and puts on* "If you want to be happy for the rest of your life, never make a pretty woman your wife."

The girls start singing as soon as they hear it, then get up and begin dancing.

KATE: Do you think Germaine Greer remembers the night she danced with her best friends in a women's dormitory at Cambridge?

RITA: No. She was probably into dating and makeup.

The girls dance and laugh.

HOLLY: Kate, you're a good dancer.

KATE: I know. I should give up law and become a rock star.

SAMANTHA: Want to see the way Robert dances? *Demonstrates as the others laugh.* It's pretty gross-me-out.

CARTER *enters and stares at them.*

CARTER: I came in to tell you I've decided what I want. I want to put Wittgenstein on film.

SAMANTHA: That's nice, Carter. Know what? We all just proposed to each other. And Kate said she'd want to marry you. Carter, Kate is really the best catch.

KATE: It was all hypothetical.

SAMANTHA: Carter, want to dance?

HOLLY: Don't you think Kate would make a great rock star?

KATE: Carter, dance with us. Just think how odd this would look if Susie Friend walked in.

CARTER *begins slowly to join them. Her dancing is noticeably different from the other girls', like a dying swan. They continue to dance and laugh.*

RITA, *over singing:* Know what? I think when we're twenty-five we're going to be pretty fucking incredible. All right, I'll give us another five years for emotional and career development. When we're thirty we're going to be pretty fucking amazing. *Pauses.* Carter, don't worry. You're younger, so you have thirteen years.

They continue to dance and sing, moving in a line toward the back of the room. HOLLY *goes to a phone in the corner. The dancing girls silhouette her from behind.*

HOLLY: Operator, could you connect me with a Dr. Mark Silverstein in Minneapolis? *Dials.* Hello, is this Dr. Silverstein? Oh, this is his answering service. Hi! A message. Respect me. I'm a respectable grown-up. Oh, my name is Simone de Beauvoir, and I should be back in an hour. *Hangs up and puts her feet on the table.*

MRS. PLUMM *enters, rapping a glass as if preparing to make an announcement. She stops at* HOLLY.

MRS. PLUMM: Holly, dear, take your feet off the furniture. *Exits.*

HOLLY *puts her feet back up and sits quietly while the music swells and the other girls continue to dance behind her.*

ACT TWO

Scene 1

HOLLY, KATE, MUFFET, SAMANTHA, LEILAH, SUSIE, *and* RITA
are ready to sing. CARTER *holds a pitch pipe. They are standing
for their performance.*

ALL:
    Mildred, Maud, and Mabel were sitting at their table
    Down at the Taft Hotel.
    Working on a plan to
    Catch themselves a man to
    Brighten up their lives a spell.
MUFFET *whispers to her friends:* I slept with a Whiffenpoof
    at the Taft Hotel.

ALL:
    In their thirty years of proms
    Never once had they had qualms
    That they could fail to satisfy their cravin'
    Nor ever seemed to doubt it's not reckless to hold out
    For a son of Old New Haven.
RITA *whispers:* These women should have been in therapy.
KATE *sings:*
        And as they downed their pousse-café . . .

Whispers: I've been here four years and I still don't know what pousse-café is.

ALL:

        The girls were heard to softly say . . .

SUSIE: I want to welcome all you fathers to Father-Daughter weekend. You dads look younger every year.

SAMANTHA: Hi, Daddy!

RITA: Hi, Mr. Stewart. *Winks.*

The girls have worked up some gestures for this part of the song.

ALL:

        Though we have had our chances
        With overnight romances
        With the Harvard and the Dartmouth male,

        And though we've had a bunch in
        Tow from Princeton Junction,
        We're saving ourselves for Yale.

RITA: Boola-Boola

ALL:

        For thirty years and then some
        We've been showing men some
        Tricks that make their motors fail.

        And though we've all had squeezes
        From lots of Ph.D.ses
        We're saving ourselves for Yale.

SUSIE: And when . . .

ALL: finally married we lie
         T'will be with an Eli . . .

SUSIE: 'Cause we're . . .

ALL: saving ourselves for Yale. For Yale!

CARTER, *raising her hand:* I knew we had a purpose.

The girls curtsy for their fathers. MRS. PLUMM *applauds and* SUSIE FRIEND *steps forward.*

SUSIE: Hi! I'm Susie Friend, coordinator of Father-Daughter weekend, and I'm delighted to see so many of you dads here. First of all, on behalf of the college, I would like to thank Holly Kaplan's father for his generous gift of two thousand slightly damaged velveteen bows. They're terrific. I'm sure they'll come in handy. Tomorrow night Mrs. Plumm has promised to play for us the white-breasted-nuthatch tapes that she made last weekend on her annual spring bird watch. And now our favorite housemother, Mrs. Plumm.

MRS. PLUMM: Welcome, fathers. This weekend has always been for me the highlight of the spring semester. My junior year, my father stopped attending Father-Daughter weekend. You see, that year, my birder classmate Ada Grudder and I had decided it was too dangerous for young girls to go on long bird-watching trips unprotected. So I wrote home asking for money to buy a rifle. Gentlemen, please don't stop me if I go on too long.

       My father was appalled. He thought firearms did not

provide an appropriate pastime for young women. And he feared I might be labeled eccentric. But I bought the rifle. Ada and I set up a firing range on Upper Lake, where we reenacted the Franco-Prussian War. For two years I received notes from home saying, "Please marry Hoyt Plumm," and "Can't you teach bird-watching at the high school?" Finally, being a dutiful daughter, I did. Now, if you will follow your daughters into the date parlor, we can begin the dance.

The girls begin to exit.

SAMANTHA: This way, Daddy.

RITA *winks again.*

MRS. PLUMM: Could you put out that cigar, dear?

Scene 2

MAN'S VOICE: In the growth of tradition from the time of its founding by Mary Lyon to the present day, the college continues to believe that the acquisition of knowledge of itself is not enough. Indeed, employers of graduates of the college seem to be looking for a readiness to work hard at learning unfamiliar techniques.

MUFFET *is putting on makeup.* LEILAH *enters carrying a chocolate bunny.*

LEILAH: Muffy, this package just came for you.
MUFFET: What is this? *She reads the gift note.* "For my Muffet.

I can't bluff it. An Easter bunny for my pixie honey."

LEILAH: Is that from Susie Friend?

MUFFET: Christ, no! It's from her father. Look, it's signed—
Lovens, E. Courtland "Kippy" Friend. He was behind me
in the bunny hop at Father-Daughter weekend. Leilah,
do you think I should plan to marry Kippy Friend? It's
two months before graduation and I still don't know what
I'm going to do next year. But I am prepared for life. I
can fold my napkin with the best of them. Leilah, do you
want this? I'll give it to Holly; she'll eat it.

LEILAH: I asked my father not to come up this year. Actually,
my freshman year he came to Father-Daughter weekend
and kept dancing with Katie and telling me how lucky I
was to have such a good friend. Kate told him I was the
prettiest and the brightest girl here. Ever since then, I've
made it a point to be busy doing research every Father-
Daughter weekend. *Throws down her books.* Oh, I can't
wait to get out of here. I've booked a flight to Iraq for
the day after graduation.

MUFFET: Really, Leilah, that's odd. You're very odd.

LEILAH: I won a fellowship.

MUFFET: Pink Pants is leaving right after graduation also. Lei,
if he calls, would you tell him I went away for the weekend? We had another fight yesterday.

LEILAH: What happened?

MUFFET: Nothing. He told me that next year he wants to
work his way around the world on a freighter. I tried to
appear like "sure," "that's fine," "have a nice trip," "send
a postcard." I don't understand why when Samantha
meets someone, suddenly she's pinned, and when I want
someone, they tell me I'm being clutchy and putting too
much pressure on them. I don't want any commitment.
I like being alone.

LEILAH: Me too.

MUFFET: Leilah, where do women meet men after college? Does Paul Weiss Rifkind have mixers with Time/Life staffers at the General Foods media department?

LEILAH: I don't know who I'll meet in Iraq. I like that. Katie says I'm escaping. I think I just need to be in a less competitive culture.

MUFFET: Why does Katie bother you so much?

LEILAH: Excuse me?

MUFFET: I can't understand why Katie bothers you so much.

LEILAH: She doesn't. I like Katie. She's exceptional.

MUFFET: Katie has no hips.

LEILAH: It could be Social Darwinism. Katie could simply be a superior creature.

MUFFET: Pink Pants says you're prettier than Katie.

LEILAH: Sometimes when I'm in the library studying, I look up and I count the Katies and the Leilahs. They're always together. And they seem a very similar species. But if you observe a while longer, the Katies seem kind of magical, and the Leilahs are highly competent. And they're usually such good friends—really the best. But I find myself secretly hoping that when we leave here, Katie and I will just naturally stop speaking. There's just something . . . *Begins to cry.* It's not Katie's fault! Sometimes I wonder if it's normal for one twenty-year-old woman to be so constantly aware of another woman. . . . "Thoughts of a dry brain in a dry season."

MUFFET: Mrs. Plumm thinks about Ada Grudder often.

LEILAH: But if we did stop speaking, she wouldn't even notice, or if she did, she'd just think she wasn't a good person for a day. I just want to get out of here so I'm not with people who know me in terms of her.

MUFFET: Leilah, why don't you come out with me tonight?

I've always wanted to do this. We can go to a bar—not too sleazy, but also not a place where two nice girls usually go. And we'll sit alone, just you and I, with our two Brandy Alexanders, and we won't need any outside attention. We'll be two Uncommon Women, mysterious but proud. *Puts her arm around* LEILAH.

LEILAH: All right. I'd like that.

MUFFET: Leilah, I do understand a little. It's debilitating constantly seeing your worth in terms of someone else.

GIRL'S VOICE: Male LD for Muffet Di Nicola. Muffet Di Nicola, Male LD.

LEILAH: I'll take it for you, Muffy.

MUFFET *pauses and then gets her coat:* No. It's got to be Old Pink Pants. Would you sign an overnight slip for me? See, Leilah, I know myself, and as soon as the phone rings, I'm just fine. *Exits with her coat.*

LEILAH *is left alone in the room holding the chocolate bunny.*

Scene 3

MAN'S VOICE: A liberal education opens out in many different directions; when intellectual experience is a real adventure, it leads toward the unfamiliar. Students at the college are expected to encounter a wide range of opportunities— that is to say, uncertainties. A maturing mind must have an ethical base, a set of values, and wonder at the unknown.

RITA, HOLLY, KATE, MUFFET, CARTER, SUSIE, *and* LEILAH *are in the living room. There is a large jar of peanut butter and*

Fluff and some crackers on the table. They are putting large globs of Fluff on their fingers and crackers.

RITA: I think if I make it to thirty I'm going to be pretty fucking amazing.

HOLLY: My mother called me today and told me she saw a 280-pound woman on Merv Griffin, who had her lips wired together and lives on Fresca. She offered me a lip job as a graduation present.

MUFFET: Pass the Fluff.

KATE: This stuff is vile. I bet the kitchen help took home the desserts.

SAMANTHA *runs excitedly into the room:* I have something to tell you. I'm getting married to Robert.

> So wave your little hand
> And whisper, "So long, dearie,"
> You ain't gonna see me anymore,
> 'Cause I'll be all dressed up
> And singing a song
> That says, "You dog"—[*Woof, woof!*]
> "I told you so . . ."
> Well, I should have said
> So long . . .

She goes into the finale: So long ago . . .

Nobody moves. Throughout the song the girls have been frozen.

SUSIE: Samantha, no.

SAMANTHA: Yes.

SUSIE: NO.

SAMANTHA: YES.

SUSIE: NO.

SAMANTHA: YES.

SUSIE: Let's run and tell Mrs. Plumm.

SUSIE *and* SAMANTHA *exit, squealing No, Yes. There is silence for a few moments.* CARTER *continues to eat.*

MUFFET: How come Carter eats so much Milk 'n' Crackers every night and never gains weight?

CARTER: I throw up immediately afterward.

Scene 4

MAN'S VOICE: The college fosters the ability to accept and even welcome the necessity for strenuous and sustained effort in any area of endeavor.

RITA *enters in denim jacket and cap:* Hey, man, wanna go out and cruise for pussy?

SAMANTHA: Beg your pardon?

RITA: Come on, man.

SAMANTHA *puts a hairbrush in her mouth as if it were a pipe:* Can't we talk about soccer? Did you see Dartmouth take us? They had us in the hole.

RITA: I'd sure like to get into a hole.

SAMANTHA: Man, be polite.

RITA *gives* SAMANTHA *a light punch on the arm:* Fuck, man.

SAMANTHA, *softly at first:* Shit, man. *Laughs hysterically.*

RITA: Fucking "A," man.

SAMANTHA: Excuse me?

RITA: Samantha, you're losing the gist.

SAMANTHA: I just feel more comfortable being the corporate type. Won't you sit down? Can I get you a drink? Want to go out and buy Lacoste shirts and the State of Maine?

RITA *picks up Samantha's bag of nuts:* Nice nuts you got there.

SAMANTHA: Thank you. You can only get them west of the Mississippi.

RITA *chews on some nuts:* I'll give you a vasectomy if you give me one.

Pause.

SAMANTHA *breaks her male character:* Rita, I liked the game when we said who we would marry much better. All right. *Goes back into character.* Anyway, I don't want a vasectomy. I like homes and babies.

RITA *picks up Piglet:* Hey, man, what's this? You got a fucking doll, man, with two button eyes, a pink little ass, and a striped T-shirt. I could really get into this. This dolly got a name, man? Piglet?

SAMANTHA: I don't know.

RITA: What's the matter, man? You afraid I think you're a pansy or something?

SAMANTHA *drops character:* Rita, cut it out.

RITA: Samantha, I'm only playing.

SAMANTHA: We're twenty-one years old, and I don't want to play.

RITA: Then why do you have the fucking doll?

SAMANTHA *takes the doll and begins to exit:* I like my doll. I've had it ever since my dad won it at the Naperville Fair when I was in sixth grade.

RITA *drops character:* Samantha, you don't like me.

SAMANTHA: I like you, Rita. We're just very different. And I don't want to play anymore.

RITA: Do you know what, Samantha? If I could be any one

of us, first I would be me. That's me without any embarrassment or neurosis—and since that's practically impossible, my second choice is, I'd like to be you.

SAMANTHA: But Rita, when you're thirty you'll be incredible.

RITA: Samantha, at least you made a choice. You decided to marry Robert. None of the rest of us has made any decisions.

Pause.

SAMANTHA: Thanks, Rita.

RITA: Well, I don't want to spend oodles of time with you. You're not a fascinating person. But I do want to be you. Very much. You're the ideal woman.

SAMANTHA: Robert says that I never grew up into a woman. That I'm sort of a child woman. I've been reading a lot of books recently about women who are wives of artists and actors and how they believe their husbands are geniuses, and they are just a little talented. Well, that's what I am. Just a little talented at a lot of things. That's why I want to be with Robert and all of you. I want to be with someone who makes a public statement. And, anyway, if I'm going to devote my uncommon talents to relationships, then I might as well nurture those that are a bit difficult. It makes me feel a little special.

RITA *takes Samantha's hand:* You *are* special, Samantha. We're all special.

SAMANTHA: It's a quiet intelligence. But I like it. Hey, Rita, when's your birthday? Because when we get out of here, we probably won't see each other very much. But I want to be sure to send you a birthday card. I like you, Rita.

RITA: It's March 28. I'm an Aries. Aries women are impulsive and daring, but have terrible domineering blocks.

SAMANTHA:

> March 28 is the day of Rita's birthday, hipooray.
> She talks of cocks and Aries blocks
> But what's so neeta about my Rita
> Is I know secretly she's very sweeta.

Pretty fucking gross, man, huh! *Gives* RITA *a light punch.*

RITA *gives her a light punch:* Yeah, pretty fucking gross, man.

They start to giggle and exit with their arms around each other.

Scene 5

MAN'S VOICE: The college maintains that, along with gaining knowledge, compassionate understanding is a central human activity.

CARTER *is sitting on the floor typing rhythmically to the "Hallelujah" chorus.* KATE *enters and turns off the music.*

KATE: Carter, do you think I'm boring? I was just reading Wittgenstein and I tried to imagine the film version. I even lit a candle and tried to imagine the film version, and all I could come up with is, you're very weird. See, Carter, you can interrupt me if you want; I've always thought it's a waste of time to scatter one's energy. I'm not saying you're wasting your time making Wittgenstein films. They're certainly not redundant, and it's a good field for women, but the possibility would never occur to me.

Carter, I'm afraid that I'm so directed that I'll grow

up to be a cold efficient lady in a gray business suit. Suddenly, there I'll be, an Uncommon Woman ready to meet the future with steadiness, gaiety, and a profession, and, what's more, I'll organize it all with time to blow-dry my hair every morning.

Tonight everything seems so programmed. Just once it would be nice to wake up with nothing to prove. Sometimes I wonder what I'd do if I didn't work or go to school. But if I didn't fulfill obligations or weren't exemplary, then I really don't know what I'd do. I have a stake in all those Uncommon Women expectations. I know how to live up to them well. I don't mind that you're not chatty. Neither am I. Did you know that I've slept with more men than Muffet or Rita? Really, it's true. I like sex with irresponsible people. It's exciting, like a trashy novel. But I couldn't live with anyone irresponsible. Gross me out.

Carter, I admire you. I really do. Sometimes I think you'll let me into your world, which is more interesting—well, more imaginative—than mine. When I'm around Holly and Muffet, I congratulate myself on being such a well-prepared grown-up. But I'm always watching myself. When I'm with you, I'm not watching myself. I feel comfortable. Isn't that odd, Carter? You're not specifically a comforting person. Maybe we have that in common. I feel as if I'm underarticulating. *Pauses.* I came in here because I just got into law school and I don't think I should go. I don't want my life simply to fall into place. Carter, can I sit here for a while? I'm frightened. CARTER *begins to put her arm around her. Kate pulls back.* No, that's all right, pumpkin. I'll just sit here for a while and then go back to work.

CARTER *goes back to her typing.*

KATE *gets up:* Why have you typed "Now is the time for all good" twenty-five times?
CARTER: I am cramming for my typing test. I need fifty words per minute to get a good job when I get out of here.

KATE *puts the "Hallelujah" chorus back on. The music swells as* CARTER *continues to type.*

Scene 6

MAN'S VOICE: The college places at its center the content of human learning and the spirit of systematic disinterested inquiry.

It is late. The girls are all studying.

KATE *looks up from her book:* Holly, did you ever have penis envy?
HOLLY: I beg your pardon?
KATE: Did you ever have penis envy?
HOLLY: I remember having tonsillitis.
KATE: Have you, Samantha?
SAMANTHA: I know I never had it. Robert's was the first one I ever saw. I didn't even know men had pubic hair.
KATE: How big is Robert's? Holly, don't fall asleep. This may be the last chance we have to accumulate comparative data. We're graduating in two more weeks. Now I remember Thomas's was around this big. That's small to medium with a tendency toward tumescence, and Iki was

around this big. But it was curved, so you can't trust my estimation. In fact, if I can remember, the others were all kind of average. Oh, yeah, except for Blaise. His really did stand out. It was the biggest I ever saw. Except it was just like him. Large, functional, and Waspy.

HOLLY: I knew a boy at Columbia with three balls. Really. He came up to see me my freshman year because his psychiatrist said I wouldn't mind.

KATE: Did you sleep with him?

HOLLY: I didn't want to hurt his feelings.

KATE: Holly, you're such a mealymouth.

HOLLY: I didn't care. I guess I don't like men's underwear. Especially when they don't remove it and it's left dangling around one ankle. In fact, if you'd like a rundown of every flaccid appendage in the Ivy League, I can give you details.

KATE: I've never been with an impotent man.

HOLLY: You haven't lived.

KATE: Listen to this! This is from a chapter in Chip Knowles' new book, *Women My Issue*. Chip has concluded that, and I quote, "the discovery at four months that a girl is castrated is the turning point in her road. At four-teen months little girls' fingers and pacifiers are intro-duced into the vagina, and at fifteen months a girl baby has been known to fall asleep with her genitalia on her teddy bear. Finally, at sixteen months they start using a pencil."

SAMANTHA: Don't little boys use pencils?

HOLLY: No. They write with their cocks.

SAMANTHA: But don't men have breast and womb envy?

KATE: Well, if they have it, they just become creative or cook dinner every now and then.

HOLLY: I guess I envy men. I envy their confidence. I envy

their options. But I never wanted a fleshy appendage. Especially a little boy's. Whenever I get fat, I get nauseated because it looks like I have one in my pants. Katie, this is nonsense. The only people who have penis envy are other men.

KATE: You mean it's all those appendages compensating for being small?

HOLLY: Yeah.

SAMANTHA: Well, I know I wouldn't want one, 'cause then I couldn't have Robert's. What time is it?

KATE: Two A.M.

SAMANTHA: I gotta go to bed. I have a History final in the morning. *Exits.*

KATE: Good night, pumpkin. *Pauses.* Holly, do you think I have penis envy?

HOLLY: Oh, Katie, gross me out!

KATE: No, really, for me it's entirely possible.

HOLLY: You don't have it.

RITA *enters, frazzled. She immediately throws herself on a bed or couch.*

RITA: You don't have what?

KATE: Nothing. Rita, what's the matter?

RITA *goes into a womb position:* I can't sleep.

HOLLY: What's wrong, Rita?

RITA: Nothing. I keep having these recurrent "Let's Make a Deal" dreams . . . and my future is always behind the curtain, and the audience is screaming at me, NO, NO! TAKE THE BOX! TAKE THE BOX! I haven't told anyone, but yesterday I went to New York, on a job interview. It was for one of those I graduated-from-a-Seven-Sister-school-and-now-I'm-in-publishing jobs.

KATE: Did you get the job?

RITA: I did very well at the interview. I told the interviewer that I was an English Composition major, and I liked Virginia Woolf and Thackeray, but what I really want is to assistant-edit beauty hints. I told her yes I thought it was so important for women to work and I would continue to write beauty hints even with a husband and family. The big thing at these interviews is to throw around your newfound female pride as if it were an untapped natural resource.

HOLLY: Did you get the job?

RITA: Holly, don't be so result-oriented. Anyway, at the end of the interview she told me it was delightful; I told her it was delightful; we were both delightful. She walked me to the door and said, "Tell me, dear, do you have experience with a Xerox machine?" I said, "Yes. And I've tasted my menstrual blood."

KATE: Rita, you didn't really do that, did you?

RITA: I did. Holly, I can't go to one of those places. I don't know what I'm going to do, but it's not going to be that. I'm not going to throw my imagination away. I *refuse* to live down to expectation. If I can just hold out till I'm thirty, I'll be incredible.

HOLLY: Rita, I think you're already incredible.

RITA: Actually, I do have a new fantasy that helps me deal with the future. I pretend that I am Picara in a picaresque novel and this is only one episode in a satiric life. *Gets up*. Hey, pumpkins, let's go down and hit the candy machine and see how much weight we can gain in a night.

KATE: All right. I should do one kinky thing before we graduate.

HOLLY: No. I have more work to do.

RITA, *triumphant again:* And when the candy machine is empty, I'm going to start writing my novel.

KATE *and* RITA *exit.*

HOLLY *puts on James Taylor's "Fire and Rain," and lies down on the bed smoking, then reaches to the telephone, dials, and puts her raccoon coat over her for comfort:* Operator, I'd like the phone number of Dr. Mark Silverstein in Minneapolis, Minn. Could you connect me with that number please? Thank you. Hello, can I speak to Mark? Oh! Do you have his number in Philadelphia? Thank you. No, that's all right. I'll call him there. *Dials again.* Hello, may I please speak to Mark? Oh, hi. My name is Holly Kaplan. I met you last summer at a museum with my friend Muffet. It was the Fogg Museum. Oh, that's all right. I never remember who I meet at museums either. *Giggles.* What's new? I'm not quite certain what I'll be doing next year. I'm having trouble remembering what I want. My friend Katie says I'm too diffuse. You'd like Katie. She's basing her life on Katharine Hepburn in *Adam's Rib.* She didn't tell me that, but it's a good illustration. No, I haven't been back to the Fogg Museum this year. My brother goes to Harvard Medical, Business, and Law schools. Maybe I'll move to Philadelphia. *Giggles.*

I'm in North Stimson Hall, fourth floor, under my raccoon coat. I guess everything's all right here. I just like being under my coat. Last week when I was riding the bus back from Yale and covering myself with it, I thought I had finally made it into a Salinger story. Only, I hated the bus, college, my boyfriend, and my parents. The only thing really nice was the coat. *Pauses.* I take that back about my parents.

Do you know what the expression "good ga davened" means? It means someone who davened, or prayed, right. Girls who good-ga-davened did well. They marry doctors and go to Bermuda for Memorial Day weekends. These girls are also doctors, but they only work part-time because of their three musically inclined children and weekly brownstone restorations. I think Mount Holyoke mothers have access to a "did well" list published annually, in New York, Winnetka, and Beverly Hills, and distributed on High Holy Days and at Episcopal bake sales. I'm afraid I'm on the waiting list. *Pauses.* You were on the waiting list for Johns Hopkins. I have a good memory for indecision. My mother says doctors take advantage unless you're thin. And then they want to marry you and place you among the good ga davened. She also says girls who have their own apartments hang towels from the windows so the men on the street know when to come up. Well my friend Alice Harwitch is becoming a doctor, and I've never seen her enter a strange building with towels in the windows. Of course, she's a radical lesbian.

Sorry to have bothered you. Hey, maybe you'd like to visit here sometime; it's very pretty in the spring. We could see Emily Dickinson's house and buy doughnuts. I think about her a lot. And doughnuts—I think about them a lot too. No, I don't write poetry, and I haven't read *The Bell Jar.* My friend Rita has. I don't know who Rita's basing her life on. Sometimes I think she'd like to be Katharine Hepburn, but Katie has the Katharine Hepburn market cornered, and we're all allowed only one dominant characteristic. I'm holding a lottery for mine. *Giggles again.* Yes, I guess I do giggle a lot, and I am too cynical. I had my sarcastic summer when I was sixteen and somehow it exponentially progressed. Leilah—she's my nice friend who's merging with Margaret Mead—says sarcasm is a defense. Well, I couldn't very well call you up and tell you to move me to Minneapolis and let's have babies, could I?

Well, sorry to have bothered you. Really, I'm fine. I find great comfort in "Lay Lady, Lay," "One Bad Apple Don't Spoil the Whole Bunch, Girl," and my raccoon coat. And I like my friends, I like them a lot. They're really exceptional. Uncommon Women and all that drivel. Of course, they're not risky. I'm not frightened I'll ruin my relationship with them. Sometimes I think I'm happiest walking with my best. Katie always says she's my best, shredding leaves and bubble gum along the way and talking. Often I think I want a date or a relationship to be over so I can talk about it to Kate or Rita. I guess women are just not as scary as men and therefore they don't count as much. *Begins to cry.* I didn't mean that. I guess they just always make me feel worthwhile. *Pauses.* Thank you. I'm sure you're worthwhile too. *Resigned.* If it's all right, I'm not going to tell Muffet I called you. Muffet's the girl who was with me in the museum. Oh, that's all right. Well, thanks for talking to me. Good-bye. Thank you. I guess so. *Lies back, turns the music back on, slides the raccoon coat over her head.*

Music swells. Lights fade out.

Scene 7

"Pomp and Circumstance" is heard under MAN'S VOICE. *The girls march in and form a line behind* MRS. PLUMM *at the tea service.*

MAN'S VOICE: Commencement brings a whole set of new opportunities, as varied as they are numerous. By the time a class has been out ten years, more than nine-tenths of its members are married, and many of them devote a number of years exclusively to bringing up a family. But immediately after Commencement nearly all Mount Holyoke graduates find jobs or continue studying. Today all fields are open to women, and more than fifty percent continue in professional or graduate school. Any one of a variety of majors may lead to a position as girl friday for an eastern senator, service volunteer in Venezuela, or assistant sales director of *Reader's Digest*.

Lights up on MRS. PLUMM, *seated in the living room.* KATE *walks up to her.*

MRS. PLUMM: What are your plans, dear?
KATE: I'm starting Harvard Law School in the fall.
MRS. PLUMM, *impressed:* Good luck, dear. *Hands* KATE *a teacup.*

KATE *sits.* LEILAH *moves up to* MRS. PLUMM.

MRS. PLUMM: What are your plans, dear?
LEILAH: I'm going to study anthropology in Mesopotamia.

MRS. PLUMM, *concerned:* Good luck, dear. *Hands* LEILAH *a cup. To* SUSIE: What are your plans, dear?

SUSIE: I'm becoming a security analyst, for Morgan Guarantee Trust.

MRS. PLUMM, *very enthusiastic:* Good luck, dear. *Hands* SUSIE *a cup.*

SUSIE *kisses her and sits.*

MRS. PLUMM: What are your plans, dear?

SAMANTHA: As you know, I'm marrying Robert Cabe. He's going to be a successful actor.

MRS. PLUMM, *hoping for the best:* Good luck, dear. *Hands* SAMANTHA *a cup.*

SAMANTHA *sits.* HOLLY *moves up to* MRS. PLUMM.

MRS. PLUMM: Holly, dear, have you thought about Katie Gibbs? It's an excellent business school. *Hands* HOLLY *a cup.* HOLLY *leaves the cup and sits.* MUFFET *enters.* What are your plans, dear?

MUFFET: I'm assuming something is going to happen to me. I figure I have two months left. *Giggles and* MRS. PLUMM *giggles.*

MRS. PLUMM: Good luck, dear.

RITA *moves up as* MUFFET *sits down; she immediately starts talking.*

RITA: Well, God knows there is no security in marriage. You give up your anatomy, economic self-support, spontaneous creativity, and a helluva lot of energy trying to convert a male half-person into a whole person who will eventually stop draining you, so you can do your own work. And the alternative—hopping onto the corporate or professional ladder—is just as self-destructive. If you spend your life proving yourself, then you just become a man, which is where the whole problem began, and continues. All I want is a room of my own so I can get into my writing. I was going to marry Clark, but he advertised himself as a houseboy in the *Village Voice* and I didn't want damaged goods. . . .

MRS. PLUMM *cuts* RITA *off:* I'm afraid our time is up, dear.

RITA *grabs a cup to toast* MRS. PLUMM, *and sits down.* MRS. PLUMM *gets up to address the audience, with the graduates sitting around her.*

MRS. PLUMM: You are all to be congratulated on your graduation. And thank you. I certainly didn't expect such an elaborate party for my retirement. I'm so glad to see so many students, faculty, and friends—and Dr. Ada Grudder, who traveled here all the way from Nagpur, India.

When MRS. PLUMM *mentions Ada Grudder, the graduates look out to the audience for her.*

MRS. PLUMM: Many memories, seasons, and teas come to mind. But I thought I'd share with you some recent thoughts. At my last Milk 'n' Crackers at the college I had an interesting talk with Kate Quin, an articulate young woman, who told me somewhat wistfully that she thought my retirement, and the recent student vote to abolish Gracious Living, marked the end of an era. I have seen the world confronting Kate and her classmates expand. The realm of choices can be overwhelming. How-

ever, those of you who have known me as the constant
dutiful daughter of my alma mater, and my family, may
be surprised to know that I do not fear these changes for
my girls, nor for myself.

My work here completed, I plan to go on a little
adventure. Next summer I will travel to Bolivia, which is
the heartland of ornithological variety on this planet. My
dear friend Ada has returned to me our trusty rifle. So
you see, girls, perhaps even I am in a transition period.

Am I cavalier about leaving Gracious Living and tea?
Hardly. You see, as a housemother and teacher, most
often I have found my work exciting. But when I grew
weary or disgruntled—I too, like Emily Dickinson, tired
of the world and sometimes found it lacking—the gentler
joys of tea, sherry, and conversation with women
friends—and I've made many good ones here—have always been for me a genuine pleasure. Thank you . . . and
good-bye.

The girls applaud MRS. PLUMM. CARTER *enters, bringing flowers.* MUFFET, KATE, HOLLY, RITA, *and* SAMANTHA *watch as*
MRS. PLUMM *exits with* CARTER, SUSIE, *and* LEILAH, *who had
gone up to congratulate her.*

Scene 8

MAN'S VOICE, *fading into woman's voice:* A liberal-arts college for women of talent is more important today than
at any time in the history of her education. WOMAN'S
VOICE: Women still encounter overwhelming obstacles to
achievement and recognition despite gradual abolition of
legal and political disabilities. Society has trained women

from childhood to accept a limited set of options and restricted levels of aspiration.

SAMANTHA: I saw Carter's Wittgenstein movie on Public Television.

KATE: Maybe I should have married Carter.

MUFFET: Leilah got married in Iraq.

KATE: You're kidding.

MUFFET: She married some Iraqi journalist-archeologist. She gave up her citizenship and converted to Muslim. She can never be divorced.

RITA: Oh, my God.

KATE: Sometimes I thought I was a bad friend to Leilah, and other times I just thought she was crazy.

RITA *touches* KATE *reassuringly.*

KATE: Rita, how's your novel coming?

RITA: Kate, do you ever have anxiety attacks? I mean the kind that give you the shits. I'm up every night till five A.M. and then I have fever dreams that I'm back in Cranfield Heights and my father has put me in the caboose of a Lionel train that goes through the Fundamentalist Church. And the men in the congregation are staring at my cunt singing—*to the melody of the familiar cat commercial*—"Meow, meow, meow, meow, meow, meow." Marilyn, my shrink, says to start slowly. So I figure if I can sleep in the morning, watch a little tube at night, I'll have it together long enough to write my novel. I figure if I can make it to forty, I can be pretty fucking amazing.

KATE: I don't know, Rita. Maybe I don't have an artistic temperament, like you and Holly. I went to see a shrink this year. A friend of Kent's.

MUFFET: Who's Kent?

KATE: The man I was sort of living with. He started objecting to my working late. I guess it never occurred to me in college that someone wouldn't want me to be quite so uncommon. Anyway, I went to see this shrink, and we had four productive sessions together and I feel fine.

MUFFET: Katie, you were all better after four sessions? You're still an overachiever.

KATE: I don't live with Kent anymore. Kent's a lovely "enlightened" man who wants to marry Donna Reed. All right, Donna Reed with an M.A. But I guess right now I'm committed to my work. *Pauses.* Muffet, do you really like insurance?

MUFFET: Wallace Stevens was in insurance. When I first took my job, I wondered what I was doing being an insurance seminar hostess. I mean, where was my prince? I guess I assumed something special would happen to me. Now I live in Hartford and I go to work every day and I won't be in the alumnae magazine like you, Katie, at the Justice Department, or Nina Mandelbaum, with her pediatric pulmonary specialty. But I never thought I'd be supporting myself, and I am.

KATE *touches Muffet's hand.*

MUFFET: Rita, I don't see how you can become strong living off Timmy. You're not doing anything.

RITA: We're suing Timmy's mother for his stocks. Actually, Kate, I was going to ask you about them. We need a good lawyer. The stocks are in his name, but in Timmy's mother's vault.

SAMANTHA: Rita, do you love Timmy?

RITA: I thought he'd be my Leonard Woolf. I just wanted to be protected, like you, Samantha. *Puts her arm around*

SAMANTHA. Samantha, you have a good marriage, don't you?

SAMANTHA: Yes, I guess I do. Sometimes I get intimidated by all of Robert's friends who come to the house. And I think I haven't done very much of anything important. So I don't talk. But Robert respects me. I don't want to sound like Mrs. Plumm, but I just want to say that I'm glad we all got together today. I had second thoughts about seeing all of you, especially Kate and Rita. Sometimes I think you might disapprove of what I do. I don't live alone, I'm not a professional, and I tend to be too polite. What I really want to tell you is, Robert and I are having a baby.

MUFFET *gets up to kiss* SAMANTHA: That's wonderful, Samantha.

RITA: Why didn't you tell us?

SAMANTHA: It's not as easy as telling you I was getting married to him. Remember when I ran into the room? Now there are more options. I decided that I was a little embarrassed to tell you, but I'm also happy.

KATE *kisses* SAMANTHA: I'm so pleased for you, Samantha, really. I even promise to sit for you on Election Day— that's my one day off. *Pauses.* I wonder if I'll ever decide to have a child. I hardly think about it, and when I do I tell myself there's still a lot of time. I wonder what it's like when you stop thinking there's a lot of time left to make changes.

SAMANTHA *smiles slightly.*

RITA: I bought the new James Taylor album last week. I put it on at five A.M. and I thought, This will be a comfort. It will remind me of my friends and I'll be able to make some connection between the past and the present. And all I heard was "Carly, I love you, darling, I do." Now how did he turn out so well adjusted? Every other person I talk to is suddenly fine and has decided to go to medical school or has found inner peace through EST. I just had hoped that at least James Taylor would hold out for something more ambiguous.

HOLLY, *who has been listening intently during the scene:* You know, for the past six years I have been afraid to see any of you. Mostly because I haven't made any specific choices. My parents used to call me three times a week at seven A.M. to ask me, "Are you thin, are you married to a root-canal man, are *you* a root-canal man?" And I'd hang up and wonder how much longer I was going to be in "transition." I guess since college I've missed the comfort and acceptance I felt with all of you. And I thought you didn't need that anymore, so I didn't see you.

KATE: Holly, I don't want to go back and have Gracious Living and tea anymore. But I still want to see all of you. We knew we were natural resources before anyone decided to tap us.

HOLLY: Let's have a toast.

SAMANTHA: All right, pumpkins. A toast to Katie's law firm.

KATE: To Robert.

HOLLY: To Rita's novel.

MUFFET: To Wallace Stevens.

ALL: To Carter.

KATE: I'm glad we decided to get together today too. I've been feeling a little numb lately. And I know I wasn't like that in college. You remember a person, don't you? I'm glad we got together too. I miss you. *Looks at all of them.* And I've got to go. I'll get the check.

SAMANTHA: We could charge it to Robert.

KATE: No. I'll take it as a tax deduction. Holly, what are you doing?

HOLLY: I keep a list of options. Just from today's lunch, there's law, insurance, marry Leonard Woolf, have a baby, bird-watch in Bolivia. A myriad of openings.

KATE: I've got to go. Kent says I dawdle. You all have my numbers.

After KATE *exits, there is silence in the room. They look at each other quietly.*

SAMANTHA: My dad was reelected mayor of Naperville.

HOLLY: My sister is marketing director of Proctor and Gamble.

RITA: Ada Grudder won the Nobel Prize. No, she didn't really. But I like to think so.

MUFFET *gets up to put on her coat:* Let's go to the movies.

SAMANTHA *gets up:* I have my car outside. Let's go see *Cries and Whispers.*

MUFFET *laughs slightly and puts her arm around* SAMANTHA: Hey, Holly, did you know Melissa Weex became a Rockette?

RITA *moves toward* HOLLY *as she puts on her coat:* Timmy says when I get my head together, and if he gets the stocks, I'll be able to do a little writing. I think if I make it to forty I can be pretty amazing. *Takes Holly's hand.* Holly, when we're forty we can be pretty amazing. You too, Muffy and Samantha. When we're . . . *forty-five*, we can be pretty fucking amazing.

They exit with their arms around each other.

END

ISN'T IT
ROMANTIC

André and Gerry made it possible for me to dedicate
this play to my parents

Isn't It Romantic was commissioned in 1979 by The Phoenix Theatre in New York. It was presented, in an earlier version, by The Phoenix Theatre, in New York City, May 28, 1981, directed by Steven Robman; the scenery was designed by Marjorie Bradley Kellogg; costumes were by Jennifer von Mayrhauser and Denise Romano; lighting by Spencer Mosse. The cast was as follows:

JANIE BLUMBERG	*Alma Cuervo*
HARRIET CORNWALL	*Laurie Kennedy*
SALVATORE	*Fritz Kupfer*
TASHA BLUMBERG	*Jane Hoffman*
SIMON BLUMBERG	*Bernie Passeltiner*
LILLIAN CORNWALL	*Barbara Baxley*
MARTY STERLING	*Peter Riegert*
PAUL STUART	*Bob Gunton*
VLADIMIR	*Fritz Kupfer*

Isn't It Romantic was presented by Playwrights Horizons, in New York City, December 15, 1983. It was directed by Gerald Gutierrez; the scenery was designed by Andrew Jackness; costumes were by Ann Emonts; lighting by James F. Ingalls; sound by Scott Lehrer; music coordination by Jack Feldman; choreography by Susan Rosenstock; J. Thomas Vivian was production stage manager. The cast was as follows:

JANIE BLUMBERG	*Cristine Rose*
HARRIET CORNWALL	*Lisa Banes*
MARTY STERLING	*Chip Zien*
TASHA BLUMBERG	*Betty Comden*
SIMON BLUMBERG	*Stephen Pearlman*
LILLIAN CORNWALL	*Jo Henderson*
PAUL STUART	*Jerry Lanning*
VLADIMIR	*Tom Robbins*
SCHLOMO STERLING	*Timmy Geissler*
HART FARRELL	*Kevin Kline*
JULIE STERN	*Swoosie Kurtz*
TAJLEI KAPLAN SINGLEBERRY	*Patti Lupone*
OPERATOR	*Ellis Rabb*
CYNTHIA PETERSON	*Meryl Streep*
CAPTAIN MILTY STERLING	*Jerry Zaks*

CHARACTERS

In order of appearance:
JANIE BLUMBERG
HARRIET CORNWALL
MARTY STERLING
TASHA BLUMBERG
SIMON BLUMBERG
LILLIAN CORNWALL
PAUL STUART
VLADIMIR

Voices
CYNTHIA PETERSON
OPERATOR
JULIE STERN
HART FARRELL
CAPTAIN MILTY STERLING
SCHLOMO STERLING
TAJLEI KAPLAN SINGLEBERRY

The play takes place in 1983 in New York City. The action is set in various locations in Manhattan, and the set should reflect the variety of locales.

In the Playwrights Horizons production, four men dressed as moving men, then waiters, joggers, and so on, shifted the sets for each scene. Thus the scene changes were incorporated into the production and often concluded during the phone-message segments.

PROLOGUE

Against the New York skyline, music and sounds of Man-
hattan fade into a voice on a phone machine. Phone-machine
segments occur between scenes. There is no action during the
prologue messages.

TELEPHONE MACHINE I

JANIE: Hi, this is Janie Blumberg. I'm not in right now, but
if you leave your name and number, I should be able to
get back to you sometime today or tomorrow. *Sings:*
"Isn't it romantic, merely to be young on such a night as
this? Isn't it romantic every something something is like
a . . ."

The machine cuts off.

Ring. Beep.

TASHA & SIMON *sing:* "Is this the little girl I carried? Is this
the little boy at play? I don't remember growing older,
when did they?" *Tasha's voice:* This is your darling
mother. I wanted to welcome you to your new apartment.
Call me, sweetheart. Your father wants to talk to you.

Ring. Beep.

HARRIET: Hi, Janie, it's Harriet. I can't help you unpack to-
      night. I have a job interview early tomorrow morning.
      Can you have breakfast with me afterward? I'll meet you
      across the street from Rumpelmayer's at ten. Oh, I ran
      into Cynthia Peterson on the street; I gave her your num-
      ber. Please don't hate me. Bye.

Ring. Beep.

SIMON: Uh, Janie, it's your father. Uh, er, uh, call your
      mother.

Ring. Beep.

CYNTHIA PETERSON: Janie, it's Cynthia Peterson. Harriet told
      me you moved to New York. Why haven't you called
      me? Everything is awful. I'm getting divorced. I'm looking
      for a job. There are no men. Call me. Let's have lunch.

Ring. Beep.

TASHA & SIMON *sing:* "Sunrise, sunset. Sunrise, sunset.
      Quickly flow the day . . ."

Dial tone.

OPERATOR: Please hang up. There seems to be a receiver off
      the hook.

ACT ONE

Scene 1

Central Park South. JANIE BLUMBERG, *twenty-eight, is sitting on a park bench. Her appearance is a little kooky, a little sweet, a little unconfident—all of which some might call creative, or even witty. There is a trash can down right.* HARRIET CORNWALL *enters from left, singing the "Charlie Girl" commercial. She could be the cover girl on the best working women's magazine. She is attractive, very bright, charming, and easily put together. She spots* JANIE.

HARRIET: I think I got the job. Hi, Janie. *Hugs her.*

JANIE: Hi, Harriet.

HARRIET: Thank God you're here.

JANIE: Of course I'm here. I got your message last night.

HARRIET: The man I interviewed with was very impressed I took a year off to look at pictures in Italy. I liked him. He was cold, aloof, distant. Very sexy. Can I have a hit of your Tab?

JANIE: Sure.

HARRIET: I can't stay for breakfast. I told him I could come right back to Colgate for a second interview. Janie, I think

our move back home to New York is going to be very
successful.

JANIE: It is?

HARRIET: Of course there's absolutely no reason why you
should believe me.

JANIE: You have an MBA from Harvard. Of course I believe
you.

HARRIET: You sound like your mother.

JANIE: No. Tasha would believe you 'cause you're thin. Look
at us. You look like a Vermeer and I look like an extra
in *Potemkin*.

HARRIET: Janie, I think someone's watching us.

JANIE *fluffs her hair:* Do I look all right? You know what I
resent?

HARRIET: What?

JANIE: Just about everything except you. I resent having to
pay the phone bill, be nice to the super, find meaningful
work, fall in love, get hurt. All of it I resent deeply.

HARRIET: What's the alternative?

JANIE: Dependency. I could marry the pervert who's staring
at us. No. That's not a solution. I could always move
back to Brookline. Get another master's in something
useful like Women's Pottery. Do a little free-lance writing.
Oh, God, it's exhausting.

HARRIET: He's coming.

MARTY STERLING *enters down left. He is Janie's mother's
dream come true: a prince and a bit of a card.*

MARTY: Hi.

HARRIET: Hello.

MARTY: You're Harriet Cornwall. I sat behind you during Twentieth-Century Problems. I always thought you were a beautiful girl. *Extends his hand.* Marty Sterling.

HARRIET *shakes it:* Hi. And this is Janie Blumberg.

MARTY: Sure. I remember you. I saw you and Harriet together in Cambridge all the time. You always looked more attainable. Frightened to death, but attainable. I'm not attracted to cold people anymore. Who needs that kind of trouble?

HARRIET: I don't know.

MARTY: So what do you do?

JANIE: Oh, I scream here on Central Park South. I'm taking a break now.

HARRIET: Janie and I just moved back to New York together. Well, at the same time. I lived in Italy for a year, and Janie was lingering in Brookline, Mass.

MARTY: Good old Brookline. Ever go to Jack and Marian's restaurant? Unbelievable kasha varnishka.

HARRIET: Excuse me?

MARTY: Kasha. Little noodle bow ties with barley. Uh, my father's in the restaurant business. Are you familiar with Ye Olde Sterling Tavernes?

HARRIET: Sure. That's a national chain.

MARTY: My father's chain.

HARRIET, *impressed:* Well!

JANIE: Well.

MARTY: Well.

HARRIET: Well.

MARTY: Well. I'm on call. I'm a doctor. Kidneys.

HARRIET & JANIE, *very impressed:* Well!

JANIE: Look, maybe you two should sit for a minute and reminisce about Twentieth-Century Problems.

MARTY: I wish I could. Good-bye.

HARRIET: Good-bye.

MARTY *starts to exit, stops, turns.*

MARTY: Janie Blumberg. Is your brother Ben Blumberg?

HARRIET: Yup. That's her brother, Ben.

MARTY: I went to Camp Kibbutz with Ben Blumberg when I was nine.

JANIE: Yup, that's my brother, Ben.

MARTY: Would you tell your brother Murray Schlimovitz says hello.

JANIE: Who's Murray Schlimovitz?

MARTY: Me. Before my father owned the Sterling Tavernes, he owned the Schlimovitz Kosher Dairy restaurants in Brooklyn. But around fifteen years ago all the Schlimovitz restaurants burned down. So, for the sake of the family and the business, we changed our names, before I entered uh . . . Harvard. Nice to see you. Bye. *Exits.*

HARRIET: What were you doing? "Maybe you two should sit and reminisce about Twentieth-Century Problems!"

JANIE: Marty Sterling could make a girl a nice husband.

HARRIET: Now you really sound like your mother.

JANIE: Hattie, do you know who that man's father is?

HARRIET: Uh-huh. He's an arsonist.

JANIE: No. He's a genius. Mr. Sterling, the little man who comes on television in a colonial suit and a Pilgrim hat to let you know he's giving away free popovers and all the shrimp you can eat at Ye Olde Salade and Relish Bar—that guy is Milty Schlimovitz, Marty Sterling's father.

HARRIET: It's all right. I can make do without Dr. Murray Marty and his father's popovers. I have to get to that

interview. My friend Joe Stine, the headhunter, says they
only have you back if they're going to hire you.

JANIE: Well, if you don't marry Marty Sterling, I'll marry
him. Wait till I tell my parents I ran into him. Tasha
Blumberg will have the caterers on the other extension.

HARRIET: I'm afraid marrying him isn't a solution. Will you
walk me back to Colgate?

JANIE: Sure. If I can get myself up.

HARRIET: Do I look like a successful single woman?

JANIE, *sizing her up:* Well.

HARRIET: What, well?

JANIE: Hattie, you know the wisdom of Tasha Blumberg?

HARRIET: Which one?

JANIE: Always look nice when you throw out the garbage;
you never know who you might meet. Put on your jacket,
sweetheart. Always walk with your head up and chest
out. Think, "I am."

HARRIET: I am. *Puts on her jacket, lifts her head and chest.*

JANIE: Now I can be seen with you. *Slumps.*

They exit arm in arm.

TELEPHONE MACHINE 2

Ring. Beep.

HARRIET: Janie, I got the job. Sorry I got you up so early. I
love you. Bye. *Sings:* "School bells ring and children sing;
it's back to Robert Hall again." Bye.

Ring. Beep.

JULIE STERN: Miss Bloomberg. This is Julie Stern at *Woman's Work* magazine. We read your portfolio. Our readers feel you haven't experienced enough women's pain to stimulate our market. Thank you.

Ring. Beep.

CYNTHIA PETERSON: Janie, it's Cynthia. There's a Lib/Men, Lib/Women mixer at the Unitarian church on Friday. It got a four-star rating in *Wisdom's Child*. My cousin Felice met an anthropologist there and she's in much worse shape than either of us. Wanna go?

Scene 2

Janie's apartment. She is asleep on the sofa. TASHA BLUMBERG *enters in a cape with an attaché case. She looks over the apartment with disdain, sets the case down on some crates, and sits next to* JANIE.

TASHA *sings and strokes Janie's hair:* "Is this the little girl I carried? Is this the little boy at play?" *Louder.* "I don't remember growing older, when did they? . . ."

JANIE, *waking up, turns and screams.*

TASHA: Good morning, sweetheart. *Kisses* JANIE. Congratulations on your new apartment.
JANIE: What?
TASHA: Your father and I came over to celebrate your new

apartment. What kind of place is this? There isn't a door-man. Is this place safe for you?

JANIE: Oh, Jesus, what are you doing here?

TASHA: I came to celebrate. You know your mother. I like life, life, life. I came over yesterday and you weren't home, so I got worried. I had the super give me the key. I thought maybe something happened with the movers.

JANIE: Nothing happened with the movers. Mother, it's seven o'clock in the morning.

TASHA: Isn't that nice? You can have breakfast with me and your father. *Opens the attaché case, turns on a Jazzercise tape, takes off her cape to reveal her tie-dyed exercise leotards, and starts to warm up.*

JANIE: What are you doing?

TASHA: I'm warming up for my morning dance class. Why don't you get up and do it with me? If you exercised, you'd have the energy to unpack your crates. *Continues to exercise.*

JANIE: Mother, I've only been here two nights. I'll unpack them later.

TASHA: Janie, people who wait, wait. I like go-go. Watch, I'll show you how to do it. *Demonstrates.* The girls at dancing school admire me so much. They tell me they wish their mothers had so much energy.

JANIE: Their mothers probably wear clothes.

TASHA: Why are you so modest?

JANIE: I'm your daughter. I shouldn't be seeing you in tie-dyed underwear.

TASHA: You're making fun of me.

JANIE: I'm not making fun of you.

TASHA, *still dancing:* One, two, three, hip. One, two, three, hip.

JANIE: Where's Daddy?

TASHA: I sent him to pick up some coffee.

JANIE: Do the girls at dancing think it's strange you order breakfast from a coffee shop every morning?

TASHA *turns off tape:* Sweetheart, when you get married, you make breakfast at your house and invite me. Anything you make will be fine. You want to make sausages, I'll eat sausages. Do you know what sausages are made of?

JANIE *lies back on sofa.*

TASHA: Janie, please don't lie there like a body. You have everything to look forward to. When you were in high school, the other mothers would stop me on the street and say, "You must be so proud of Janie. She's such a brilliant child. If only my daughters were like Janie."

JANIE: What are the names of these mothers? I want names.

Doorbell rings.

TASHA: There's your father with the coffee. *Opens door.* SIMON BLUMBERG, *Tasha's partner, a very sweet father, though not chatty, enters with a bag containing coffee and a sandwich.*

SIMON: Janie, is this place safe for you? There isn't a doorman. Why don't you put in the lock I bought you in Brookline?

JANIE: I left it there.

SIMON: You left it in Brookline? That lock cost fifty dollars.

JANIE: I have it, Dad. I have it.

SIMON: You want to split this egg sandwich with me?

TASHA: Simon, please, there's a proper way to do this. First we have to toast Janie's new apartment. *Hands out the coffees.* I remember my first apartment in New York. Of course, I was much younger than you and I was already married to your father. *Toasts:* To Janie. Congratulations, welcome home, and I hope next year you live in another apartment and your father and I have to bring up four coffees.

JANIE: You want me to have a roommate?

TASHA: I want you to be happy. Talk to her, Simon, like a father with a daughter. Maybe she wants to tell you her problems.

JANIE: I don't have any problems. How's the business, Dad?

SIMON: Your father always with the business, right? You want to see something, Janie? *Pulls out an envelope.* Smell this.

JANIE *smells the envelope:* It's nice.

SIMON: I can't make them fast enough. And then those jerks ship me a million envelopes without any perfume. You know what that's going to do to the Valentine season? Your father always with the headaches.

JANIE: It's all right, Dad. I like the envelope. Smells like the State of Maine.

SIMON: You want to come down to the business today and see whether it interests you? Then I'll take you skating after work.

JANIE: I can't, Dad. I have to follow up some leads for clients here. Some other time I'd like to. *Puts on a sweatshirt over her flannel nightgown.*

TASHA: Is that an outfit! Simon, from a man's point of view, is that what you'd call an appetizing outfit?

SIMON: If you were a lawyer, like your brother, Ben, then it makes sense to go out on your own. But I don't understand why a girl with your intelligence should be freelance writing when you could take over a business.

TASHA: Christ is thinking of going to law school when the children get a little older.

JANIE: Who?

TASHA: Your sister-in-law, Christ.

JANIE: Chris, Mother! It's Chris. I'll come down and see your place next week, Dad. I promise.

SIMON: Take your time, honey. Whenever you're ready.

TASHA: My two big doers. If not today, tomorrow. I can't sit like you two. *Dances.* One, two, three, hip. One, two, three, hip. *Goes over to* JANIE.

JANIE *turns away:* I won't dance. Don't ask me.

TASHA: Look at those thighs. I'm dying.

SIMON: What's-his-name called our house last night looking for you.

TASHA *stops dancing:* Who? Who?

SIMON: The popover boy. He called Ben, because they went to summer camp together. And Ben didn't have your new number, so he told him to call us.

JANIE: Ben told Marty Sterling to call you?

TASHA: Please, sweetheart, look nice. It's important. Even when you throw out the garbage. I like this Marty Sterling.

JANIE: You don't even know him.

TASHA: He comes from nice people.

JANIE: His father is an arsonist.

SIMON: Believe me, you can have a nice life with him. Sounds like a very nice boy. He said to give you a message to call him at the hospital. He was in the Emergency Room at Mount Sinai.

TASHA: I told you he was a nice boy.

JANIE: Don't get too excited. He probably wants Harriet's number.

TASHA: What does Harriet have to do with the popover boy?

JANIE: He's *her* friend.

TASHA: Why do you belittle yourself all the time? What kind of attitude is that? Why don't you walk into a room with your head up and your chest out and think, "I am." *Demonstrates.* Am I right, Simon?

SIMON: What is it?

TASHA: Sweetheart, stop thinking about those envelopes and look at your daughter. From a man's point of view, isn't that some beautiful face?

JANIE: I am beautiful. People stop each other on the street to say how beautiful I look when I throw out the garbage. And when Marty Sterling proposes, he'll say, "Janie Jill Blumberg, I want to spend the rest of my life with you because every member of your family calls me the popover boy and I want to be near your mother in her tie-dyed underwear."

TASHA: She's making fun of me again.

JANIE: I'm not making fun of you. It's good to be home. *Kisses them.* If I was still in Brookline—what time is it? Seven-fifteen—if I was still in Brookline, I'd be sleeping. Here, by seven-fifteen, there's a catered meal and a floor show.

TASHA: The girls at dancing say you can always have a good time with Tasha. Honey, it was wonderful to see you. Thank you for having us, I loved your cooking, and I'm sure you'd like me to stay and chat all day, but your father isn't the only one who has to get to work. I'm demonstrating in class today.

SIMON: Have a nice day, Janie. *Kisses* JANIE *and starts to exit.*

TASHA: Where are you going? Give her some money so she'll buy a lock.

SIMON *gives* JANIE *some bills:* Honey, I'm sorry if I seem preoccupied. Mother walks me to work every morning now. Once I walk a few blocks, my mind gets stimulated. You know, Janie, I used to have the same trouble with my legs as you do. I would have to sit in bed and rest all the time. But you know what makes the difference? Ripple soles. You get a pair of shoes like these and then you're in business. *Gives* JANIE *more bills.*

JANIE: Thanks, Daddy.

TASHA: So you'll call this Marty Sterling?

JANIE *pats Tasha's head:* I will call him. I will call him.

TASHA: Am I getting shorter? I'm getting shorter.

JANIE: You're fine, Mother. *Flops back on sofa.*

TASHA: Body, please, don't get back into bed. You have everything ahead of you. You can have a family, you can have a career, you can learn to tap-dance!

JANIE: Are you taking tap dancing?

TASHA: It's part of life. I'll teach you. *Taps quite smoothly, calling out the steps,* "Flap, heel, flap, touch."

SIMON, *while* TASHA *dances:* I told your mother she could run her own dancing school.

TASHA, *ending dance:* Two lessons. *Puts on her cape and takes her attaché case.*

SIMON: Don't you think your mother looks nice? That's a new attaché.

TASHA: I'm an executive mother.

JANIE: It looks very nice.

TASHA: You want it?

JANIE: You keep it, Mother.

SIMON: Let's go, dear. Remember, Janie, ripple soles. *Exits.*

JANIE *flops back on sofa again and sighs.*

TASHA: Janie, please! Only old ladies sigh. *She sighs and exits.*

Scene 3

Lillian Cornwall's office. LILLIAN CORNWALL, *an impressive, handsome woman, whose demeanor commands respect, is seated behind her desk. She is speaking on the phone.*

LILLIAN: Obviously, Dick, our only choice is to go national with this. I don't care what some kid in your department says about numbers. Hold on a minute, will you? *Pushes a button on the phone.* Lillian Cornwall. *Yells offstage.* Pauline, no one's picking up the phone here. *Hits another button.* Dick, trust me on this one. I'm not being too harsh. No, I didn't think so. Thank you. *Hits another button.* Lillian Cornwall's office. *Yells offstage.* Pauline! *Back on the phone:* I'm sorry, Mrs. Cornwall isn't in. Can I take a message? Oh, Dick, it's you. Well, tell the kid in your department I appreciate his confidence. What can I say? I'm a beautiful, successful, brilliant woman. Dick, I'm simply not a kid. *Phone buzzes.* Hold a sec, will you? *Pushes another button.* Yes, Pauline. *Pushes another button.* Dick, my lovely daughter is here. Gotta go.

Hangs up. HARRIET *enters in a stylish business suit. She is carrying a gift box.*

HARRIET: Hello, Mother.
LILLIAN: Hello, baby. It's nice to see you.

They kiss.

HARRIET: You're looking well.

LILLIAN: What brings you here? Would you like me to order you a salad or some lunch? I'd call Tom and get us into Four Seasons, but I have a meeting in a few minutes.

HARRIET: That's all right. I have to get back to the office. Ummmm. *Takes out three noisemakers and blows them as she hands* LILLIAN *the present.* Happy birthday, Mother!

LILLIAN: Hmmmm?

HARRIET: Happy birthday. I bought this for you in Italy before I ran out of money.

LILLIAN: Oh, God, I bet that meeting is a birthday thing. Thank you, Harriet. It's very handsome. *Puts the gift back in the box.* How are things at Colgate?

HARRIET: Fine.

LILLIAN: Don't say fine, Harriet. You're a Harvard MBA. I expect an analysis.

HARRIET: We're changing the test market from Sacramento to Syracuse.

LILLIAN: Makes sense. And your personal life?

HARRIET: Mother!

LILLIAN: I don't have much time to catch up. I have a meeting.

HARRIET: My personal life is okay.

LILLIAN: Is that better or worse than fine?

HARRIET: It's okay. Janie's back in New York, and that's nice. I see my friend from Harvard, Joe Stine, the headhunter.

LILLIAN: Nice boy.

HARRIET: Nice. A little dull.

LILLIAN: Sweet though. No, you're right. A little dull.

HARRIET: And I'm sort of interested in some guy in my office.

LILLIAN: Is that a good idea?

HARRIET: I'm not seeing him. I'm just attracted to him.

LILLIAN: Sounds like a pleasant arrangement. What does he do?

HARRIET: Mother!

LILLIAN: His job, baby! What does he do?

HARRIET: He does all right. He's my boss's boss.

LILLIAN: How old is he?

HARRIET: Around forty.

LILLIAN: Around forty? He should be further along than your boss's boss.

HARRIET: Happy birthday, Mother.

LILLIAN: Harriet, you can ask me questions about my life right after I'm finished with yours. You're not making this easy, baby.

HARRIET: Sometimes you're hard to take, Mother.

LILLIAN: So they say. *Answers intercom:* Bill, I'll be there in a minute. My daughter is with me. Can she be present at this meeting? I thought so. Thanks, Bill. *Hangs up.* It *is* a birthday thing. Harriet, why don't you come with me? You can be my date.

HARRIET: Mother, do you remember when you took me to group sales meetings in Barbados? And I appeared in Mary Janes as your date at candlelit dinners by the ocean.

LILLIAN: You were a wonderful date. Interesting, attractive, bright. Certainly more suitable than what was available.

HARRIET: Mother, you're so crazy. I hope I'm going to be all right.

LILLIAN: You'll be fine. Don't dwell on it. Your generation is absolutely fascinated with itself. Think about science. Technology is going to change our world significantly. So, do you want to come?

HARRIET: Sure.

LILLIAN: God, I dread going to this kind of thing.

HARRIET: Me too.

LILLIAN: I'm not being too harsh?

HARRIET: No, you're not being too harsh.

LILLIAN: Comb your hair, baby. I like it better off your face.
Pushes Harriet's hair off her face.

Scene 4

Italian restaurant. MARTY *and* JANIE *are seated. "Volare" is playing in the background.*

MARTY: Do you want dessert? Because if you don't like the dessert here, my father is giving away free popovers in the Paramus Mall. So what do you think you're going to do now?

JANIE: With my life? At this restaurant? Tonight?

MARTY: Now that you've come home.

JANIE: I don't know. Retire. I sent away for some brochures from Heritage Village.

MARTY: I think about retirement. Not that I don't like being a doctor, but I don't want to get trapped. You know what I mean? First, you get the Cuisinart, then the bigger apartment, and then the Mercedes, and the next thing you know, you're charging $250 to Mrs. Feldman, with the rash, to tell her, "Mrs. Feldman, you have a rash."

JANIE: Whenever I get most depressed, I think I should take charge of my life and apply to medical school. Then I remember that I once identified a liver as a heart. Really. I demonstrated the right auricle and the left ventricle on this liver.

MARTY: I left medical school after my first year to do carpentry for a year.

JANIE: Your father must have liked that.

MARTY: He wants me to be happy. I'm very close to my parents.

JANIE: That's nice. *Pauses.* I'm sorry. I was thinking about my parents.

MARTY: Are you close to them?

JANIE: In a way. She's a dancer and he's very sweet. It's complicated.

MARTY: My father started out in show business. He used to tell jokes at Grossinger's. That's why he does the popover commercials himself. Now he's the toastmaster general for the United Jewish Appeal.

JANIE: Have you ever been to Israel?

MARTY: I worked on a kibbutz the second time I dropped out of medical school. Israel's very important to me. In fact, I have to decide next month if I want to open my practice here in New York or in Tel Aviv.

JANIE: Oh.

MARTY: Why, are you anti-Israel?

JANIE: No. Of course not. I just preferred the people my parents' age there to the younger ones. The people my age intimidated me. I'd be sleeping and they'd go off to turn deserts into forests. The older ones had more humanity. They rested sometimes.

MARTY: I think Jewish familes should have at least three children.

JANIE: Excuse me?

MARTY: It's a dying religion. Intermarriage, Ivy League colleges, the *New York Review of Books. Pauses.* So, how's Harriet?

JANIE: She's fine.

MARTY: She's not sweet, like you.

JANIE: Harriet is wonderful.

MARTY: She's like those medical-school girls. They're nice but they'd bite your balls off. You think Israelis have no sense of humor? Believe me, women medical students are worse. *Takes Janie's hand.* Janie, you're one of the few real people I've ever met in a long time. Most of the women I meet aren't funny.

JANIE, *quickly:* Marty, I think I should tell you I find the fact that you don't like women doctors extremely disturbing and discriminatory. I support the concept of Israel and would probably be a much happier, healthier person if I could go out into the desert and build a forest, but I am far too lazy and self-involved. I have very fat thighs, and I want very badly to be someone else without going through the effort of actually changing myself into someone else. I have very little courage, but I'm highly critical of others who don't.

MARTY, *sweetly:* Is that it?

JANIE: And I want you to like me very much.

MARTY: Do you like me?

JANIE: Yes.

MARTY: Sounds tentative. Most women fall in love the minute they hear "Volare." Maybe this will help. I bought it for you when I was in Rome. *Hands* JANIE *a swizzle stick.*

JANIE: I was wondering why they have swizzle sticks in the wine.

MARTY, *à la the Godfather:* I got connections in the restaurant business. *Takes Janie's hand.* Should I take you home, Monkey?

JANIE: What?

MARTY: Want to go home?

JANIE: No. My interior decorator is there.

MARTY: Want to come to my parents' house? They should be out late tonight. After Paramus, there's a UJA testimonial dinner for my father. It means a lot to him, because he's been giving away so much shrimp at the salad bar they almost revoked his job as toastmaster.

JANIE: It's weird going to someone's parents' house. Shouldn't we have mortgages and children?

MARTY: Let's go, Monkey. You'll be all right. I'll help you. *Takes Janie's hand.*

JANIE *rises:* And what'll I do for you?

MARTY *rises:* Be sweet. I need attention. A great deal of attention.

Lights fade as MARTY *embraces* JANIE.

Scene 5

Harriet's apartment. HARRIET *and* PAUL STUART *enter.* PAUL *is about forty. He looks very corporate and appealing.* HARRIET *takes their coats and tosses them on a chair. She exits into the kitchen.* PAUL *moves to the sofa, takes out Binaca, gives himself a hit, and sits.* HARRIET *enters, pushing a rolling bar.*

PAUL: You remind me a lot of my first wife.

HARRIET: Mr. Stuart, would you like something to drink? I don't have much. I just moved here.

PAUL: Scotch on the rocks. My first wife hated office Christmas parties.

HARRIET: I'm sorry. Did I make you leave?

PAUL: Definitely not. You're one of the most amusing people I've met at Colgate in a long time. Can I tell you something as a friend? You don't have to call me Mr. Stuart.

HARRIET: I think it's funny your name is Paul Stuart. If your name was Brooks Brothers, I'd call you Mr. Brothers. *Hands him a napkin, with a cracker and a plate.* Pâté?

PAUL *takes it:* Where are you from originally? *Cracks up.* Have you ever noticed when you try a conversation opener like "Where are you from originally?" you always sound like a jerk?

HARRIET: I grew up in New York. My mother still lives on East 69th Street.

PAUL: East 69th Street. You were a rich kid.

HARRIET: No. Upper middle class.

PAUL: Only rich kids know what upper middle class is.

HARRIET: Well, I wasn't spoiled. Definitely not spoiled.

PAUL: Your father was a lawyer?

HARRIET: No. My mother's an executive.

PAUL: Is your mother Lillian Cornwall?

HARRIET: Yup.

PAUL: Jesus. I interviewed with your mother once. That woman has balls. Do you know what it took for a woman in her time to get as far as she did?

HARRIET: Yup.

PAUL: Poor baby, I bet you do. *Lights her cigarette.* Would you like me to spoil you a bit? Relax. For a girl with such a good mind, you get tense too easily.

They both start laughing.

PAUL: Why are you laughing?

HARRIET: You're amazing. First you tell me how amusing I am, then you want to spoil me, and now you tell me what a good mind I have. What are you doing to do next? Ask me to come up and see your etchings?

PAUL *moves away to his drink.*

HARRIET: I'm sorry. This is making me a little uncomfortable. Office romance and all that. You're my boss's boss.

PAUL: Harriet, do you know that forty percent of the people at McKinsey are having interoffice affairs?

HARRIET: How do you know that?

PAUL: Friend of mine did the study. Look, I live with a woman, so no one will know. Is that an incentive?

HARRIET: Cathy? Do you live with Cathy?

PAUL: How do you know Cathy?

HARRIET: She calls the office three times a day.

PAUL: You've been paying attention.

HARRIET: I'm a smart kid.

PAUL *pinches* HARRIET: Smart woman.

HARRIET *pulls away:* Paul, I generally try not to get involved with unavailable men.

PAUL: You've never been with a married man? How old are you? *Chokes and coughs.*

HARRIET: Are you all right?

PAUL: Jesus, were there any nuts in that pâté? My doctor told me not to eat nuts. I've got this stomach thing. I tell you, Harriet, when you get older you really gotta watch it. But you'll take good care of me, right, Beauty? *Pauses.* Are you excited?

HARRIET: Where are you from originally?

PAUL: You're excited. Don't be embarrassed, Beauty. I'll be wonderful for you, Harriet. You'll try to change me, you'll realize you can't and, furthermore, I'm not worth it, so you'll marry some nice investment banker and make your mother happy.

HARRIET: I don't think my mother particularly wants me to get married. I don't particularly want me to get married.

PAUL: You'll change your mind. Career girls, when they hit thirty, all change their minds. Look, whatever is happen-

ing here, we better do it quickly, because Cathy is expecting me home with the laundry at eleven. I'm very
attracted to you, Harriet.

HARRIET: Forty percent of the people at McKinsey, huh?

PAUL: And those are just the ones crazy enough to fill out the
questionnaire.

HARRIET: Get out of here.

PAUL: C'mere. Deal from strength, Harriet. Men really like
strong women. *Pulls* HARRIET *toward him. There is no
struggle.*

Scene 6

JANIE *is in her apartment, typing. The doorbell rings. She
opens the door.* HARRIET *enters with a package.*

HARRIET: Congratulations on your new apartment!

JANIE: Harriet, I've been living here three months.

HARRIET: That's why I came to celebrate. I decided this morning it was time for you to unpack. Did I walk in with my
right foot first?

JANIE: I don't know.

HARRIET: Then I have to do it again. *Exits, rings doorbell,
and reenters when* JANIE *opens the door.* Congratulations
on your new apartment!

JANIE: What are you doing?

HARRIET: I looked all this up very carefully in the *Oxford
Companion to Jewish Life.*

JANIE: I'm not familiar with this companion.

HARRIET: You have to walk into a new apartment with your
right foot, to set you off on the right foot. I also brought

you a housewarming gift. But you cannot open it till we get you settled in.

JANIE: Harriet, you know I can't postpone gratification.

HARRIET: Janie, you have to make a home for yourself. Now, what are we doing to do with these crates? *Picks up two crates.*

JANIE: Harriet, what are you doing? You're flying around the room.

HARRIET *exits with the crates:* It's Saturday.

JANIE: The day of rest. Didn't they tell you that in the *Oxford Companion*?

HARRIET: It's Paul Stuart's day at home with Cathy. You want me to put the typewriter in the bedroom? *Picks up the typewriter.*

JANIE *stops her:* No. I'm working. Marty's father hired an actor to play a popover at the opening of the new Sterling Taverne, in the Green Acres Mall, and Marty got me a job writing the popover's opening remarks. Hattie, don't you mind not seeing Paul on the weekend?

HARRIET: No, it's okay. As I see it, Paul Stuart is fine until I find the right relationship. It's similar to the case method. And he's great in bed.

JANIE: Marty claims he slept with more than a hundred visiting nurses when he was at Harvard.

HARRIET *sits:* Really!

JANIE: I just told you that so you'd sit down. *Sits too.*

HARRIET: So, is it something with Marty?

JANIE: He decided to open his practice here next month and he's invited me to his parents' house for Chanukah. Some days I walk down the street and think if I don't step on any cracks, I'll marry Marty. What ever happened to Janie Blumberg? She did so well; she married Marty the doctor.

They're giving away popovers in Paramus. *Pauses.* Hattie, do you think I should marry Marty?

HARRIET: I've always hated women who sit around talking about how there are no men in New York. Or everyone is gay or married.

JANIE: What does this have to do with my marrying Marty?

HARRIET: These women would tell you, "Marry him. He's straight, he'll make a nice living, he'll be a good father." Janie, what women like Cynthia Peterson don't understand is, no matter how lonely you get or how many birth announcements you receive, the trick is not to get frightened. There's nothing wrong with being alone.

JANIE: Harriet, do you remember when we used to listen to "My Guy" and iron our hair before going to a high-school dance?

HARRIET: Oh, God, I've blocked all of that.

JANIE: I remember arriving at the dance, looking over the prospects, and thinking: When I'm twenty-eight, I'm going to get married and be very much in love with someone who is poor and fascinating until he's thirty and then fabulously wealthy and very secure after that. And we're going to have children who wear overalls and flannel shirts and are kind and independent, with curly blond hair. And we'll have great sex and still hold hands when we travel to China when we're sixty.

HARRIET: I never thought about any of that. Maybe it's because I'm Lillian's daughter, but I never respected women who didn't learn to live alone and pay their own rent. Imagine spending your life pretending you aren't a person. To compromise at this point would be antifeminist—well, antihumanist—well, just not impressive. I'm not being too harsh?

JANIE: No. Just rhetorical.

Doorbell rings.

HARRIET: Who's that?
JANIE: I don't know. *Answers door.*

VLADIMIR, *about thirty, a Russian taxicab driver enters, holding a bar with a safari motif.*

VLADIMIR: Hello, hi.
JANIE: Do you have the right apartment?
VLADIMIR: You are Miss Bloomberg?
JANIE: Yes.
VLADIMIR: For you. I am Vladimir. I am filmmaker from Moscow. I drive taxi now. *Enters with bar, sees* HARRIET. Hello, hi.
SIMON *enters with bar stool:* Janie, do you like this bar? Hello, Harriet. We thought you might need something to entertain with at home.
TASHA *enters with another stool:* Don't force her, Simon. Hello, darling. *Notices* HARRIET. Harriet, you look terrific. Are you seeing anyone?
HARRIET: Sort of.
SIMON: We met Vladimir on the cab ride down here. He came from Moscow six weeks ago.
JANIE: That's nice. Do you like it here?
VLADIMIR: Hello, hi.
SIMON: He doesn't speak very much English.
TASHA: That doesn't matter. If you like people, you speak every language. I can get along in any country. If you smile, you dance, anyone will understand.
JANIE: My mother identifies with Zorba the Greek.
VLADIMIR: Zorba. Yes. Thank you.
TASHA: Harriet, do you like the bar? I saw another one, but

I was afraid Janie would say it's too old, it's too new, it's gold.

HARRIET: I like it very much. It's primitive.

SIMON: Vladimir, maybe you want to stay and put the bar together, and Mrs. Blumberg and Harriet and I can bring you up some coffee.

VLADIMIR: Coffee. Regular.

TASHA: Sit. Harriet, join us. Harriet's with Colgate-Palmolive.

SIMON *takes* JANIE *aside:* He's a nice boy. Don't you think he's a nice boy, Janie? Seems intelligent too. I thought maybe if things didn't work out with you and Marty, I'd take him into the business.

JANIE: You're kidding. This man is here six weeks and he gets a wife, a business, and a dancing mother-in-law?

SIMON: What's wrong with giving a guy a break?

JANIE *makes a sign to get* VLADIMIR *out:* Dad . . .

SIMON: Vladimir, thank you. We'll take the taxi uptown to Rockefeller Center.

TASHA: Every Saturday I take Mr. Blumberg skating.

SIMON: My partner keeps me in shape.

TASHA: Harriet, you look terrific. Who is it you're seeing?

JANIE: She's seeing someone who's married.

TASHA: Let's go, dear.

TASHA *and* SIMON *exit.*

HARRIET & JANIE: Good-bye. Good-bye. Nice to see you.

VLADIMIR, *to* HARRIET: Good-bye. *To* JANIE: Good-bye. *Exits.*

JANIE: One of these days, I'm going to write a book: *My Mother Herself.* I'm sorry, Hattie. That was the only way I could get them out of here.

HARRIET *looks at the bar:* Did Tasha go on safari?

JANIE: No. She went hunting at K Mart. Harriet, they brought over a Russian taxicab driver for me to marry! Maybe I should move back to Brookline tomorrow.

HARRIET: You can't leave me here with Lillian and Paul Stuart. I gave Lillian a birthday present that I bought with my last lire in Italy. She hardly opened it. She couldn't wait to get back to the intercom to harass Pauline. Janie, sit; it's the day of rest. It's time for you to open your present.

HARRIET gives her the bag, and they sit on the sofa. JANIE puts the bow on her head and from the package takes out a loaf of challah bread, a box of kosher salt, sugar, matches, and a candle.

JANIE: What kind of diet are you on?

HARRIET: According to the *Oxford Companion*, this is what your family brings when you move into a new home. Bread—the staple of life. Sugar—something sweet in your life. Salt—a little spice in your life.

JANIE, *looking at the bar:* I have that.

HARRIET: And a candle to light the way. *Lights the candle.* Janie, you know what I remember more than those mixers?

JANIE: What? *Puts her arm on Harriet's shoulder.*

HARRIET: Remember when you and I would meet for dinner because Lil was at a meeting and Tasha only had brewer's yeast in the refrigerator. I always thought, Well, I do have a family. Janie's my family. In fact, that still helps a lot. I always assumed it was some sort of pact.

JANIE: It is a pact.

Both break a piece of bread from the loaf.

JANIE: Hattie, thank you for my gift from my family. *Picks up the salt as if toasting.* Cheers.

HARRIET *picks up the sugar:* Lechayim.

They clink the boxes together.

TELEPHONE MACHINE 3

Ring. Beep.

HART FARRELL: Janie Blumberg, this is Hart Farrell, in the personnel department at Sesame Street. A temp in our office recognized your name from a part he played at Green Acres Mall. I read your pieces. I'm going to pass them on to Tajlei Kaplan Singleberry. Nice song, luv.

Ring. Beep.

CYNTHIA PETERSON, *crying:* Janie, it's Cynthia. Thank God you have your machine on. I'm home, I'm broke, my trainer is on retreat, I've been rejected by every man on the Upper West Side, and I'm about to get drunk. Janie, do you know a good dry cleaner?

Scene 7

Janie's apartment, left: sofa and TV on a crate. Harriet's living room/bedroom, right: foldout bed, ottoman, TV. PAUL *and* HARRIET *are in bed. Light goes up on Janie's apartment.*

JANIE *enters:* I fucked up Chanukah.

MARTY *enters:* You were sweet.

JANIE: I'm sorry I spilled horseradish on your sister-in-law. They have a nice baby. Really, Schlomo is very sweet. I'm sorry I spilled horseradish on Schlomo.

MARTY: You worry too much. You're just like my mother. My mother says you're shy and a little clumsy because you're very angry with your family. But she says don't worry, you'll grow out of it. I told her your mother was a bit cuckoo.

JANIE: Martin, I'm reflective and eager to please, and my mother is a pioneer in interpretive dance. *Exits into bedroom.*

MARTY: Don't be so defensive, sweetheart.

JANIE, *offstage:* Everything by you is so simple.

MARTY: Everything by you is harder than it has to be. You think my sister-in-law knew what she was doing when she married my brother?

JANIE *enters. She has changed from her dress into sweatshirt and overalls.*

MARTY: That didn't come out right, did it?

JANIE: That's okay.

MARTY: You know what I mean. My sister-in-law had even less direction than you do, and she's a bright girl too. But she met my brother and now she's a wonderful mother, and, believe me, when Schlomo is a little older, she'll go back to work in something nice. She'll teach or she'll work with the elderly—and she won't conquer the world, but she'll have a nice life. Monkey, I don't want to be alone. But I think it's going to be all right with us. I love you.

Pauses. I put a deposit down on an apartment for us in
Brooklyn today.

JANIE: What?

MARTY: I figured if I waited for you to make up your mind
to move, we'd never take anything, and I need a place to
live before I open my practice. You don't have to pay
your half of the deposit now. I can wait a month. Is that
okay?

JANIE: Sure.

MARTY: I decided we should live in Flatbush or Brighton
Beach, where people have real values. My father never
sees those people anymore, the alta kakas in Brooklyn,
the old men with the accents who sit in front of Hymie's
Highway Delicatessen. I miss them. My father and mother
never go to Miami anymore. They go to Palm Springs or
Martinique with their friends from the Westchester Country Club. My father thought my brother was crazy when
he named his son Schlomo. He kept asking my brother,
"So what's his real name?" And my father will think I'm
crazy when we move to Brooklyn.

JANIE: Marty?

MARTY: What is it, Monkey? Are you angry?

JANIE: No. I like the alta kakas in Brooklyn too. I always
thought Herman Wouk should write a novel, *Young
Kaka*. I don't know.

MARTY: What don't you know? Janie, you're twenty-eight
years old. What I'm saying is, either you want to be with
me—you don't have to; you should just want to—or, if
you don't want to, then we should just forget it.

JANIE: I want to.

MARTY: So, what's the problem?

JANIE: No problem.

MARTY: Uh-oh. What time is it? I promised my father we'd watch his new commercial. *Turns on the TV.*

PAUL *turns on the TV at the same time.*

HARRIET: I know that man.

VOICE-OVER: This is your Captain Milty Sterling. I'm here at beautiful Green Acres Mall with the popover boy and my grandson, Schlomo. What are we giving away today, Schlomo?

CHILD'S VOICE-OVER: We're giving away shrimp. We're giving away lobster tails. We're giving away coleslaw.

MILTY VOICE-OVER: How do you like that shrimp, Schlomo?

CHILD'S VOICE-OVER: It's good, Grandpa.

ANNOUNCER: Sterling Tavernes are now located in Green Acres, Syosset, Paramus, Albany, Plattsburgh, Marine Park, Midwood, Madison, Bethesda, and the Bergen Mall.

Lights fade on MARTY *and* JANIE *and come up on* PAUL *and* HARRIET.

HARRIET, *laughing hysterically:* I can't believe I know him!

PAUL: Why are you laughing? The man's a marketing genius. He's giving away shrimp. He's giving away coleslaw. I never heard of such an incentive program. How much do you think he can give away and still make a profit? *Kisses* HARRIET. It's good, Grandpa. *Gets up.*

HARRIET: Where are you going?

PAUL: It's late.

HARRIET: You could spend the night.

PAUL: Cathy.

HARRIET: Do you love Cathy?

PAUL: She's devoted to me.

HARRIET: Does Cathy exist?

PAUL: Of course Cathy exists.

HARRIET: I thought maybe Cathy was an answering service you hired to call you three times a day.

PAUL *sits back on the bed:* Did I tell you to deal from strength?

HARRIET: Yes.

PAUL: Sometimes I'm a jackass. You're sweet, Harriet. You know that? You're a sweet woman. A lot of people never get off in their entire life. Do you think your mother's had good sex?

HARRIET: My mother likes to watch "The Rockford Files" reruns at eleven. *Gets out of bed.* Paul, I don't think people spend as much time thinking about sex as you do.

PAUL *follows her:* Tell me what you like, Beauty.

HARRIET: The other day I was standing in front of your office with my PERT charts, and you called your secretary "Beauty," you called whoever called you on the phone "Beauty," and I think you called the ninety-year-old messenger boy from Ogilvy and Mather "Beauty."

PAUL: I see what's going on here. It's the old "I'm afraid of turning thirty alone and I'm beginning to think about having a family."

HARRIET: Wanting two nights a week or a sleepover date isn't quite a family.

PAUL: Baby, I'm older than you. I've been through this with a lot of women. You want a man who sees you as a potential mother, but also is someone who isn't threatened by your success and is deeply interested in it. And this man should be thought of as "intelligent" by your friends. But when you need him, he should drop whatever it is he's doing and be supportive.

HARRIET: I'm not asking for that. Why are you so bitter?

PAUL: Don't be naïve. Everything is a negotiation, Harriet. Everything. When I graduated from Yale, I thought I'd find a nice wife who would cook me dinner, we'd have a few kids, and I'd support the family; and a few years up we'd get a house in Madison, Connecticut, for weekends. The girl I married never cooked, and she wasn't lucky, like you. Girls didn't assume they'd have careers then. My wife was just very bright and very unhappy. And the girls I date now—the ones like you, the MBAs from Harvard—they want me to be the wife. They want me to be the support system. Well, I can't do that. Harriet, I just wasn't told that's the way it was supposed to be.

HARRIET: Paul, I never knew which way it was supposed to be.

PAUL: What do you mean?

HARRIET: I don't really expect anything from you.

PAUL: You and I are a lot alike, Harriet. We don't want to be alone and we don't want to move forward. So we serve a perfect function blocking each other's lives.

HARRIET: I like you, Paul.

PAUL: My poor baby.

They kiss and get back in bed as the lights fade down on them and up on JANIE *and* MARTY.

MARTY: I'm hungry. What do you have to eat, Monkey?

JANIE: We could order up a sandwich. I have the phone number of every coffee shop on the Upper East and West Sides—Four Brothers, the Four Brothers on the Acropolis, the Four Brothers on the Parthenon, the Four Brothers . . .

MARTY *cuts her off:* That's all right, I'll go to the supermarket, get some chicken and some lettuce and stuff.

JANIE: No, no, no. We can order up a salad.

MARTY: Monkey, you don't know how to cook a chicken?

JANIE: I do. I do. I do. I can make Teflon chicken.

MARTY: You shouldn't put yourself down like that. *Gets up to go.*

JANIE: Marty, I love you. We can take the place in Brooklyn. I just want to be with you.

MARTY *kisses* JANIE, *crosses to the front door, and exits triumphantly.* JANIE *goes to phone and dials. The phone rings in Harriet's apartment.* HARRIET *picks it up.*

HARRIET: Hello.

JANIE: Hattie, how do you cook a chicken? Marty's coming back here in five minutes with a chicken.

HARRIET: Do you want Florentine or something nice?

JANIE: Hattie, hurry. I can't tell him I don't know how. Marty took an apartment for us in Brooklyn, and I can't tell him we have to order up chicken.

HARRIET: Why Brooklyn?

JANIE: He likes Hymie of Hymie's Highway Delicatessen.

HARRIET: Excuse me?

JANIE: He likes the alta kakas.

Janie's doorbell rings.

JANIE: Marty, just a sec. Hattie, how do you cook a chicken?

PAUL *gets up:* Beauty, do you have any Di-gel?

HARRIET: In the cabinet.

JANIE *crosses to the door.*

HARRIET: Janie, what are altered kakas?

JANIE *opens the door.* VLADIMIR *is there.*

VLADIMIR: Hello, hi. I am in neighborhood. So I drop in. Want to see *The Sorrow and the Pity?*
JANIE, *into phone:* Hattie, I have to go. Vladimir is here. He wants to see *The Sorrow and the Pity.* When can I see you?
HARRIET: I don't know. I don't have my book here.

Janie's doorbell rings.

PAUL: What's wrong with this mouthwash?
HARRIET: It's a Colgate product.

VLADIMIR *answers the door.* SIMON *enters with a coffee table.*

SIMON: Oh, hello, Vladimir. How are you?
VLADIMIR: Fine. Thank you. How's it going?
SIMON: Janie, I brought over a coffee table.
PAUL: I better go, Beauty. Cathy.
HARRIET: Me too. "The Rockford Files."

MARTY *enters with a bag of groceries.* PAUL *and* HARRIET *engage in a long kiss.*

MARTY: Monkey, I got the chicken.
JANIE: Marty, this is my father, Simon Blumberg, and Vladimir.
SIMON: Very nice to meet you. Mrs. Blumberg will be so sorry she missed you.
JANIE, *desperately, into phone:* Harriet!
VLADIMIR: Hello, hi.
SIMON, *to* MARTY: Vladimir is *my* friend. Janie doesn't even

know him. He's a filmmaker from Moscow. Let's go, Vladimir. *Starts pulling* VLADIMIR *out the door.* Nice to meet you. My best to your family.

PAUL, *at Harriet's door:* I think we have a pretty good thing going. Think about it.

PAUL, SIMON, *and* VLADIMIR *exit simultaneously.*

HARRIET: Janie!

MARTY: Who's the filmmaker?

JANIE: Friend of my father's.

MARTY: I'm hungry. Are you sure you can cook a chicken? *Hands* JANIE *a chicken wrapped in butcher paper.* I'll go warm up the oven.

JANIE: I'll get the stapler. *Back on the phone, as* MARTY *exits into the kitchen:* Hattie!!

HARRIET: Janie, you never mentioned an apartment. When did you see it?

JANIE: I haven't seen it. Marty told me about it tonight after I spilled horseradish on baby Schlomo.

HARRIET: Janie, people named Homo and Schlymie! I feel our move back to New York has been very successful. I've met a sadist vice president and you've become involved in a shtetl.

MARTY, *offstage:* Monkey!

JANIE: Be right there, Marty. *With desperation.* Hattie, *how do you* cook a chicken?

HARRIET: You just put it in the broiler.

JANIE: Who told you this? Thank you, Harriet. Bye. *Hangs up.*

HARRIET: Bye, Janie.

JANIE *unwraps the chicken on the coffee table. She lifts it up by the two wings, over her head, and stares at it.*

PAUL *enters:* Beauty, Thursday the laundry's open till midnight.

MARTY *enters:* Janie, the oven's ready.

JANIE *and* HARRIET *cross to* MARTY *and* PAUL *respectively as the lights fade.* JANIE *cradles the chicken like a baby;* HARRIET *is carried off by* PAUL. *Both couples kiss as they exit. A string version of "Isn't It Romantic" is heard.*

ACT TWO

Scene 1

Central Park South. TASHA *enters wearing earphones connected to a Walkman tape player. She is listening to music that makes her dance as she walks. She sits on a bench, opens her attaché case, and wipes her face with a towel.* LILLIAN *enters, eating a hot dog, and sees* TASHA.

LILLIAN: Mrs. Blumberg?

TASHA *doesn't hear her.*

LILLIAN: Mrs. Blumberg!

TASHA, *loudly:* Yes.

LILLIAN: Lillian Cornwall.

TASHA *removes her earphones:* How are you? Please excuse my appearance. I just got out of class. A real workout I had today.

LILLIAN: You look marvelous. How's Ben?

TASHA: Ben is doing very well. He's a lawyer with Korvette's. I mean Cravath.

LILLIAN: And Simon?

TASHA: Simon is with his business. He would love for Janie

to take over, but Janie says she's happy free-lance writing.

LILLIAN: I always liked Janie. She's such a bright girl.

TASHA: I tell her people stop me on the street to tell me how bright she is, but she doesn't believe me. Janie tells me Harriet has a nice job.

LILLIAN: Yes. She's at Colgate-Palmolive.

TASHA: She going to be an executive mother, like you. Very nice. Do you see the girls much? My daughter, whenever I call her, I get the machine.

LILLIAN: I reach Harriet's secretary, or, rather, my secretary reaches Harriet's secretary.

TASHA: She's always been a hard worker, your Harriet.

LILLIAN: Harriet tells me Janie's been seeing a nice boy.

TASHA: He's a very nice boy. But so what? Harriet and Janie are very nice girls. They deserve a little *naches*. You know what I mean by *naches*? A little happiness. Well, I don't want to keep you. I know you're a busy woman. You probably have appointments.

LILLIAN: Actually, I thought I'd surprise Harriet and take her to a nice lunch, but her secretary told me she was in a meeting. So I thought I'd treat myself to a frankfurter in the park. I haven't had a frankfurter in the park since I lived in England, thirty years ago.

TASHA: Can I tell you something? I'm sorry, I forgot your first name.

LILLIAN: Lillian.

TASHA: Lillian, maybe it's none of my business, but you shouldn't eat frankfurters. You know what frankfurters are made of? Have some string beans. *Takes a bag of string beans from her attaché case.* All the young girls at dancing school carry plastic bags with string beans.

LILLIAN *takes a bean:* Thank you.

TASHA *sits and sighs:* Excuse me. I always tell my daughter only old ladies sigh. My husband has an expression, "Everything presses itself out." Believe me, Harriet will find a nice boy, she'll get married, she'll work, she'll have a nice life. I don't understand why they're fighting it so hard.

LILLIAN: I don't think Harriet thinks about marriage very much.

TASHA: These days they "live together." That's the latest. Believe me, it's the same thing as being married.

LILLIAN: Harriet told me she doesn't particularly want to live with anyone. I don't live with anyone.

TASHA: You can't listen to your children all the time. My daughter tells me I don't wear clothing. I'm wearing clothing. My daughter, Janie, thinks I call her in the morning to check up on her. Yesterday she answered the phone and said, "Hello, Mother. This morning I got married, lost twenty pounds, and became a lawyer."

LILLIAN: That's funny.

TASHA: Oh, you can always have a good time with Janie. But you know what's sad? Not sad like a child is ill or something. But a little sad to me. My daughter never thinks I call because I miss her. The girls at dancing school tell me their problems: they tell me about their parents, their boyfriends, what they ate yesterday, what they're going to eat tomorrow. But they're not my children. Sure, I'd like Janie to be married, and if she were a lawyer that'd be nice too, and, believe me, if I could take her by the hand and do it for her I would. I'm that sort of mother. I remember when Janie was in high school and she'd slam the door to her room and say, "Mother, what do you want from me?" Lillian, what do I want from her? I just want to know that she's well. And to give her a little push too. But just a little one.

LILLIAN, *reassuringly:* Sooner or later you can have everything pressed.

TASHA: It's "everything presses itself out." I tell you, life isn't like those Ivory Snow commercials with the mother and daughter comparing hands. Maybe your life is like that, but at seven-fifteen in the morning, my Janie and I don't get up to play golf together.

LILLIAN: Harriet and I don't get up to play golf either. *Pauses.* Do those string beans really fill you up?

TASHA: You're an intelligent woman, Lillian; how could a bag of string beans really fill you up?

LILLIAN: Do you ever go to Rumpelmayer's, across the street?

TASHA: I take my granddaughter when she's in the city.

LILLIAN: Rumpelmayer's always sold the nicest stuffed animals. I never liked those Steiff toys at F.A.O. Schwarz.

TASHA: They're made in Germany.

LILLIAN: How many grandchildren do you have?

TASHA: Just one. But I'm looking forward. I'll tell you what's nice about grandchildren. You don't have to worry about them every day, and they don't *hoc* you a *chinic*. That means they don't bang on your teakettle.

LILLIAN: Would you join me at Rumpelmayer's for a sundae? I have twenty minutes before I have to go to a meeting. I'm sure you can get an iced coffee and some fruit.

TASHA: Why should I have fruit when they have such nice ice cream? I don't care what restaurant you go to, the fresh fruit cup is never fresh.

LILLIAN: I haven't gone for a sundae in the afternoon since I was at Vassar. This is a big day for me. A frankfurter in the park, a sundae at Rumpelmayer's. I'm having a wonderful time.

TASHA: The girls at dancing school always say you can have a good time with Tasha.

LILLIAN: Do you like James Garner?

TASHA: Who?

LILLIAN: Do you ever watch "The Rockford Files"?

TASHA: I put the television on sometimes when I'm waiting for Simon to come home after my classes, but I don't really watch it. Just educational broadcasting and the Barbara Walters' specials. Did you see her with Richard Nixon the other week? That man did all right for himself.

LILLIAN: I beg your pardon?

TASHA: Both his daughters married well, he has a nice house, he travels. And what was he before? A Quacker.

LILLIAN: Excuse me?

TASHA: A Quaker. Listen, I know you people don't like to get very intimate, but since our daughters are such good friends, I want to tell you I always admired you. You were always on time to all the parent-teacher meetings. Not that you and I both aren't smarter than all those teachers combined. But the other mothers would always come in late with the Louis Vuitton bags, and the manicures, but you, the only one who had something else important to do, you were always on time.

LILLIAN: Thank you.

TASHA: What are you thanking me for? You worked very hard. We both worked very hard. That's why we put out such nice products.

They walk off arm in arm chatting.

TASHA, *as she exits:* Do you remember that girl Cynthia Peterson?

TELEPHONE MACHINE 4

Ring. Beep.

TAJLEI KAPLAN SINGLEBERRY: Miss Bloomberg, this is Tajlei Kaplan Singleberry, at "Sesame Street." Could you come in and see us next week? 288-7808, extension 22. Thank you.

Ring. Beep.

HARRIET: Janie, it's Harriet. Would you do me an enormous favor? Would you and Marty come to dinner tomorrow night? Paul Stuart will be there. Don't ask. *Sings:* "I love him. I love him. I love him. And where he goes I'll follow, I'll follow, I'll follow. . . .

Scene 2

Harriet's apartment. JANIE, MARTY, *and* HARRIET *are having drinks.*

HARRIET: My mother identifies with Jean Harris.
JANIE: I think Jean's mistake was stopping with Dr. Tarnower. On her way to Scarsdale she should have taken care of all of them: Dr. Atkins, Dr. Pritikin, the nut in Beverly Hills who says it's good to live on papaya.
MARTY: Monkey, Jean Harris should stay in jail for life. *His beeper goes off.* I hear you, Mrs. Rosen. I hear you. *To* HARRIET: I was up all night with her. She thinks the

dialysis machine is connected to my telephone. Do you
have a private one I could use?

HARRIET: In the kitchen.

As MARTY *exits, he looks back at* JANIE.

HARRIET: He's sweet.

JANIE: He's very sweet. Sometimes I look at Marty and think
he's such a nice young man, I must be a nice young girl.

HARRIET: You are.

JANIE: I never meant to become one. Last week, when we
were driving up from yet another Sterling Taverne opening on the Island, I had my head in his lap, and he stroked
my hair and called me Monkey. And at first I thought,
Janie Jill Blumberg, you've been accepted; not even on
the waiting list. So he calls you Monkey. You'd prefer
what? Angel? Sweetheart?

HARRIET: Beauty?

JANIE: And I thought, It's settled, fine, thank God. And I bet
I can convince him that Schlomo is not a name for an
American child. We were driving along the L.I.E. I was
fantasizing if we'd make the Sunday *Times* wedding announcements: "Daughter of Pioneer in Interpretive Dance
Marries Popover Boy." And it was just as we were approaching Syosset that I thought, I can't breathe in this
car, and I promised myself that in a month from now I
would not be traveling home from the Island in this car
with Marty. And as soon as I thought this, and honestly
almost pushed open the car door, I found myself kissing
his hand and saying, "Marty, I love you." I don't know.

HARRIET: I don't know either. Maybe Lillian is right. Maybe
life is easier without relationships.

JANIE: Hattie, do you think I should live with Marty?

HARRIET: Well, if you live with him, you won't have to wonder who'll hold you at night, what will happen if you
don't pay your taxes, or even, if you want children, who
you could possibly get to be the father. You won't read
articles in magazines about single women and have to
think of the fifty different reasons why you're different
from that. You won't begin to notice younger men on the
street, or think I'm not really hurting a married man's
wife if I have an affair with him, because if it's not me,
it'll be somebody else. But Janie, how could you sleep
next to a man as nice as Marty and lie to him and say I
love you?

JANIE: I do love him. Maybe I'm just frightened.

HARRIET: I thought we had a pact. There's nothing wrong
with being alone. We can wait till it's right.

MARTY *enters.*

HARRIET: How's Mrs. Rosen?

MARTY: She died. . . . Just kidneying. Actually, she's not happy
with her donor, so I'm driving her home to Rye.

HARRIET: Oh, I'm going up to Rye next week for a planning
conference. My friend Joe Stine is driving me up there.

Doorbell rings.

HARRIET: Maybe we can take Mrs. Rosen with us. *Goes to
the door.*

MARTY: Actually, I can't stay for dinner. The hospital wants
me back in a half hour. *To* JANIE: Who's Joe Stine?

JANIE: Some friend of Harriet's. I've never met him.

PAUL *enters. His shoulder is held stiff against his ear.*

PAUL: I think I got whiplash on the cab ride down here.

HARRIET: I'm sorry. Are you all right?

PAUL: There's no way to get around safely in this city. God-damn taxi driver went over a pothole.

JANIE: Do you want Marty to have a look at your neck?

PAUL: It's not my neck. It's my left arm. Oh, my God. Maybe I'm having a heart attack.

MARTY: Really, I don't mind having a look at it.

JANIE: Marty's a resident at Mount Sinai.

PAUL: Nice to meet you. *Shakes his hand.*

MARTY: And this is Janie Blumberg.

PAUL: The only other possibility is, my doctor says I've been taking too many amateur massages.

HARRIET: Paul, how about a drink?

PAUL: I better not, with this neck thing.

MARTY: I can recommend a chiropractor.

JANIE: I thought chiropractors were quacks. My mother says chiropractors are quacks. She's a dancer.

PAUL: Your mother's a dancer? What company is she with?

JANIE: She's an independent.

HARRIET: Sweet gherkins? Paul, remember the TV commercial we saw? Well, Marty's father's the one who was giving away the shrimp.

PAUL: Oh, I loved it. I loved it. Is that kid's name really Schlomo?

MARTY: Yes. The UJA is really pissed at my father for making Schlomo eat shrimp on television.

PAUL *cracks up:* I love it. I love it.

HARRIET: More Brie, Marty? *To* PAUL: How are you feeling?

PAUL: I don't know, honey. I have this sensation in my foot. Maybe this is a neurological thing.

JANIE: Well, maybe.

MARTY: Doesn't seem to be.

PAUL: What's your specialty?

MARTY: Kidneys.

PAUL: The kid's name is really Schlomo? *He cracks up again.*
    I love it.

JANIE: You're in marketing, aren't you?

PAUL: Yes. But it's too boring to talk about.

HARRIET: I don't think it's boring. *To* MARTY: Have some
    gherkins?

Pause.

PAUL: Anyone seen anything good recently?

MARTY: God, I haven't been to a film in ages. If I get any
    time, I try to read.

JANIE: Did you read the article in the *Times* about artificial
    insemination? I can imagine myself at thirty-six, driving
    cross-country to inseminate myself with a turkey baster.

PAUL: Turkey baster?

JANIE: Uh-huh. I'm going to give birth to a little oven-stuffer
    roaster.

JANIE, MARTY, *and* HARRIET *laugh.*

PAUL *gets up:* Well, I have to be going.

JANIE: Aren't you going to stay for dinner? There's chicken
    Marengo.

MARTY: Really, I wouldn't rush off because of the whiplash.

PAUL: Nice meeting both of you. Cathy, er, Beauty, I'm just
    a little tired. *Kisses* HARRIET *on the cheek, picks up his
    coat, and starts to leave.*

HARRIET: Paul, I don't think we should see each other any-
    more.

PAUL *stops.*

PAUL: Excuse me?

HARRIET: I want to stop.

PAUL *moves down to* HARRIET *and whispers:* We've been through this before.

MARTY: Harriet, do you want Janie and me to get dessert?

HARRIET: No.

PAUL: C'mon, Harriet. I've got this neck thing. Your friends are here. We'll talk about it tomorrow. We'll have breakfast. What's the matter, Beauty, do you have your period?

MARTY *stands, with* JANIE: See you later.

HARRIET: Don't go.

They sit.

HARRIET: Paul's leaving to catch up on his laundry.

PAUL: You knew what the parameters were here. You're a very appealing woman, Harriet. It's nice meeting both of you. Thanks for helping me with this neck thing. Beauty, calm down. You're a good kid. *Snaps his fingers as if to say "see you later" and exits.*

MARTY: He's crazy. He didn't have whiplash. Harriet, he's the least gracious man I ever met. In fact, he's a real douche.

JANIE: Hattie, I'm sorry.

HARRIET: What are you sorry for?

JANIE: I shouldn't have told him about artificial insemination.

HARRIET: I'm going for a walk.

JANIE: When are you coming back?

HARRIET: Janie, you sound like Tasha. I don't know when I'm coming back. *Exits through the front door.*

JANIE: Well, this was a real nice clambake. I'm mighty glad *I* came.

MARTY: Why is she seeing that guy?

JANIE: The sadist vice president at Colgate-Palmolive? I don't know.

MARTY: Monkey.

JANIE: What?

MARTY: My father wants to know if we're coming to dinner tomorrow. It's my brother's anniversary. The whole family will be there.

JANIE: I can't. I got a call from "Sesame Street." They want to interview me. I have to stay home and put together some sketches for the giant bird.

MARTY: So you'll do it next week. What?

JANIE: Nothing.

MARTY: What nothing, Monkey?

JANIE: Nothing. Nothing.

MARTY: You want to interview at "Sesame Street," fine. They do nice work. But don't let it take over your life. And don't let it take over our life. That's a real trap.

JANIE: Marty, I haven't even interviewed there yet.

He rubs her back intermittently, tapping as if he's checking her heart.

MARTY: You're a sweet woman. You don't want a life like that.

JANIE: Like what?

MARTY: Look, I have plenty of friends who marry women doctors because they think they'll have something in common. Monkey, they never see each other. Their children are brought up by strangers from the Caribbean.

JANIE: That's a nice way of putting it.

MARTY: I have nothing against your working. I just want to make sure we have a life.

JANIE: Marty, I like my work. I may have stumbled into something I actually care about. And right now I don't want to do it part-time and pretend that it's real when it would actually be a hobby. But I want a life too. Honey, my mother takes my father skating every Saturday. Simon and that dancer have struck up a partnership. I'm their daughter. I want that too.

MARTY: Janie, I made arrangements with the Sterling truck to move us to Brooklyn next Saturday.

JANIE: We're gonna move with a lot of shrimp and lobster tails?

MARTY: What are you trying to do, entertain me like you tried to entertain Paul Stuart?

JANIE: I was just trying . . .

MARTY: You know what, Monkey? You're a little disorganized; I'm a little bit of a nudge. So if I don't make the arrangements, what's going to happen? You'll live alone or maybe you'll meet someone who's even more of a nudge.

JANIE: Marty, if I'm one of the few real people you've ever met, why do you call me "Monkey"?

MARTY: Jesus, Janie, I'm just trying to move forward. I gotta go. I'm on call this week. I'll see you on Saturday.

Snaps his fingers as if he's imitating PAUL *and exits.* JANIE *walks around the sofa, slowly turns, and gasps.*

TELEPHONE MACHINE 5

Ring. Beep.

VLADIMIR: Hello, hi. This is Vladimir. Hello, hi. Uh, I have tickets for Bruce Springsteen. I will return call.

Ring. Beep.

CYNTHIA PETERSON: Janie, it's Cynthia Peterson. I met a man on a plane to Houston. Keep your fingers crossed.

Scene 3

Four Seasons restaurant. HARRIET *and* LILLIAN *are seated at a table. They have finished their entrées.* HARRIET *is distracted.*

LILLIAN: Everything all right with you?
HARRIET: Fine. I guess. I made a presentation to my boss a week ago. He told me my ideas were too theoretical. Then the next day, at a meeting, my friend Joe Stine said, my boss presented my ideas as his own and got them through.
LILLIAN: Good for you.
HARRIET: Mother, I work very hard. I don't want that man stealing my ideas.
LILLIAN: You think it would be better to be married and have your husband steal your ideas?
HARRIET: What?
LILLIAN: I was just cheering you up with a depressing alternative. Look at Jean Harris. That guy would have manipulated her for the rest of her life. Do me a favor, baby. Go in tomorrow and tell your boss, whoever he is—Ron, Rick, Dick—I am sorry but you stole my ideas, and I hold you accountable. Do you want dessert? Have some chocolate velvet cake, and I'll take a taste.
HARRIET: Mother, you haven't finished not eating your lunch.

You haven't picked all the salad dressing off your salad
or removed all the potatoes from your plate.

LILLIAN: Tom, we'll have the chocolate velvet cake.

HARRIET: I remember when you brought me here as a little
girl. I told everyone in my class we were going to the Four
Seasons for lunch, because you told me it was very special.
I always loved coming here, and I thought you were very
beautiful in your subtle blue suits, calling all those grown
men Tom, Dave. I mean, they never really knew the other
women in the room, but they knew my mommy. My
mommy was important.

LILLIAN: She is. Harriet, you can't blame everything on me.
I wasn't home enough for you to blame everything on
me.

HARRIET: Clever.

LILLIAN: I thought so. *Waves to someone.* Hi, Bill.

HARRIET: Are you proud of me?

LILLIAN: Of course I'm proud of you. Are you proud of me?

HARRIET: Yes. Very.

LILLIAN: I didn't cheat you too much.

HARRIET: No.

LILLIAN: Have children, Harriet. It's one of the few things in
life that's worthwhile. *Waves at another man.* Hi, Kip.

HARRIET: Mother, when do you stop hoping that there will
be some enormous change, some dam breaking, and then
you'll start living your life? You know what I'm tired of?
I'm tired of the whole idea that everything takes work.
Relationships take work, personal growth takes work,
spiritual development, child rearing, creativity. Well, I
would like to do something simply splendidly that took
absolutely no real effort at all.

LILLIAN: Harriet, your thinking is all over the place today.
What is it? Are you having an affair or something?

HARRIET: My boss's boss. The one you said should be further along. But it's nothing.

LILLIAN: Forty percent of the people at McKinsey are having affairs.

HARRIET: I know that.

LILLIAN: See how nice it is to have a daughter in your own field? If you want me to, I'd like to meet this guy.

HARRIET: It's over. He once had an interview with you. He said you have balls.

LILLIAN: Don't be offended, baby. Your father said the same thing. *Waves again.* Hi, Ken. Where's our cake? I have a meeting at two-thirty.

HARRIET: Mother . . . ?

LILLIAN: What is this, "Youth Wants to Know"? Honey, I'm an old lady. I don't know all the answers to these things.

HARRIET: I have just one more question. Just one.

LILLIAN: To get to the other side.

HARRIET: What?

LILLIAN: I was giving you the answer.

HARRIET: That's not funny.

LILLIAN: I'm not a funny woman. Ask me, baby. I've got to go. Where is that man? I can't sit around here like this.

HARRIET: Calm down.

LILLIAN: What's your question? Harriet, I'm in a hurry.

HARRIET: Mother, do you think it's possible to be married or live with a man, have a good relationship and children that you share equal responsibility for, build a career, and still read novels, play the piano, have women friends, and swim twice a week?

LILLIAN: You mean what the women's magazines call "having it all"? Harriet, that's just your generation's fantasy.

HARRIET: Mother, you're being too harsh. Listen to me. What

I want to know is if you do have all those things—my generation's fantasy—then what do you want?

LILLIAN: Needlepoint. You desperately want to needlepoint. *Pauses.* Life is a negotiation, Harriet. You think the women who go back to work at thirty-six are going to have the same career as a woman who has been there since her twenties? You think someone who has a baby and leaves it after two weeks to go back to work is going to have the same relationship with that child as someone who has been there all along? It's impossible. And you show me the wonderful man with whom you're going to have it all. You tell me how he feels when you take as many business trips as he does. You tell me who has to leave the office when the kid bumps his head on a radiator or slips on a milk carton. No, I don't think what you're talking about is possible.

HARRIET: All right. When you were twenty-nine, what was possible for you?

LILLIAN: When I was your age, I realized I had to make some choices. I had a promising career, a child, and a husband; and, believe me, if you have all three, and you're very conscientious, you still have to choose your priorities. So I gave some serious thought to what was important to me. And what was important to me was a career I could be proud of and successfully bringing up a child. So the first thing that had to go was pleasing my husband, because he was a grown-up and could take care of himself. Yes, baby, everything did take work; but it was worthwhile. I never dreamed I'd be this successful. And I have a perfectly lovely daughter. Baby, I have a full, rich life.

HARRIET: Mommy, what full, rich life? You watch "Rockford Files" reruns every night.

LILLIAN: If a man more appealing than James Garner comes

into my life, I'll make room for him too. Okay, baby?

HARRIET: Well, I've made up my mind. I'm going to try to do it: have it all.

LILLIAN: Good for you. For your sake, I hope you can. *Pauses.* What's the matter, Harriet? Did I disillusion you?

HARRIET: No. I'm afraid I'm just like you.

LILLIAN: Don't be afraid. You're younger.

HARRIET: Mother, you're trying my patience.

LILLIAN: You sound just like me, dear.

HARRIET: If you were younger, I'd say something nasty.

LILLIAN: Whisper it late at night. It will give you guilt and anxiety. Your sweet old mom who worked for years to support you.

HARRIET: Fuck off, Mother.

LILLIAN: Don't tell that to your boss. Pay the bill, will you? Comb your hair, baby. I like it better off your face. Call me Sunday. Pretend it's Mother's Day. *To waiter:* This young lady will take the check, please. I love you, Harriet. *Kisses her on the cheek.*

HARRIET: I love you too.

LILLIAN: Sometimes.

HARRIET: Sometimes.

LILLIAN, *as she exits:* Lovely lunch, Tom. Thank you.

HARRIET *sits alone at the table and takes out her American Express Gold Card. She lays it on the table.*

TELEPHONE MACHINE 6

Ring. Beep.

SIMON: Janie, it's Dad. Do you want to meet us at Oscar's for brunch?

Ring. Beep.

MARTY: Monkey, sweetheart, are you there? Pick it up. Pick it up. I have to do my father a big favor tomorrow in Central Park. You and I will have dinner in Brooklyn.

Scene 4

Central Park. Sousa's "Washington Post" is heard. MARTY *enters, to cheers. He picks up a mike. Camera flashes go off.*

MARTY, *into microphone:* This is Dr. Murray Schlimovitz, standing in for my father, Captain Milty. I'm here at beautiful Central Park to inaugurate the first annual Sterling Marathon. That's right. He's giving away spring water, he's giving away seltzer, he's giving away carob bars.

JANIE *enters left.*

MARTY: And you know what my father always says: "You should only live and be well." *Waves, as the crowd cheers, puts down mike, and moves to* JANIE. Janie?
JANIE: Hi, Dr. Murray Schlimovitz.
MARTY: I decided to open my practice in Brooklyn under my real name. What are you doing here?
JANIE: I was in the neighborhood. They accepted my sketches for the giant bird. Does Mount Sinai know you're here?

MARTY: I'm here because it's my responsibility to my family. *Pauses.* Oy, I'm such a schmucky nice doctor.

JANIE: You're not such a schmucky nice doctor. What's the matter?

MARTY: I don't understand you. I call you all last night to coordinate the time for the moving truck to arrive at your house today. You don't return my calls, and then you arrive here today ready to crack jokes. Janie, what are you, a home-entertainment unit? Honey, go home. The moving truck will be at your house in an hour.

JANIE: Marty, do you ever get the feeling that everything is changing and you don't know when you decided to make the change?

MARTY: Nothing's changing. I'm offering you love, I'm offering you affection, I'm offering you attention. All you have to do is put your crates that you never unpacked on that truck and get on the Belt Parkway. You just move forward.

JANIE: I can't just move forward.

MARTY: You know what I think? I think you're frightened to try. You think it's a compromise. You think you're not grown-up yet. That's bullshit. Maybe you think I'm not special enough.

JANIE: I think you're very special. But I want us to decide to move when we decide together. Marty, you took an apartment and you didn't even tell me about it first. None of it had anything to do with me. I don't want to sneak around you and pretend that I'm never angry. I don't want to be afraid of you. I guess to a man I love I want to feel not just that I can talk, but that you'll listen.

MARTY: Do you think I don't listen to you?

JANIE: You have all the answers before I ask the questions.

MARTY: You picked a hell of a time to bring this up. You

want to give the answers, fine. You make the decision right now. Either you move in with me tonight or we stop and I'll make alternate arrangements.

JANIE: Marty, by you everything is much more simple than it has to be. You want a wife; you get a wife. You drop out of Harvard twice; they always take you back. You're just like me. We're too fucking sweet. I'm so sweet I never say what I want, and you're so sweet you always get what you want.

MARTY: Not necessarily. Why do you think I'm thirty-two and not married? All I want is a home, a family, something my father had so easily and I can't seem to get started on. Why? I'm a nice Jewish doctor. Women want to marry their daughters off to me all the time. Sure, I want to know where I'll live, who'll take the children to the nursery, but I wanted something special too. Just a little. Maybe not as special as you turned out to be, but just a little. Janie, I don't want to marry anyone like my sister-in-law.

JANIE: I never liked her. Honey, I wish we could throw a wedding at the Plaza. And your father could be toastmaster general, and Harriet would select my pattern, and my mother would dance, and baby Schlomo could carry the ring in one of my father's gold-seal envelopes.

MARTY *cuts her off suddenly, quite angry:* Goddammit, Janie, make a decision! You want to have children with a turkey baster, that's fine. You want to write sketches for a giant bird at two o'clock in the morning, that's fine too. You want to come home to Cynthia Peterson's phone calls, great. You want to find out what it's like to take care of yourself, good luck to you. But it isn't right for me. And I'll tell you something, Janie: it isn't right for you either.

JANIE, *softly:* Marty, you're not right for me. I can't move in with you now. If I did that, I'd always be a monkey, a sweet little girl.

MARTY, *after a pause:* I have to get back with the starting pistol.

JANIE *stops him:* Honey, it's complicated.

MARTY: No. It's simple. You don't love me enough. *Exits.*

JANIE: Marty . . . .

JANIE *is left alone as* MARTY, *speaking through a microphone, is heard offstage.*

MARTY: This is Dr. Murray Schlimovitz, at the first annual Sterling Marathon. Runners ready. On your mark. Get set. Go.

JANIE *is left alone on the stage as lights fade.*

TELEPHONE MACHINE 7

Ring. Beep.

HARRIET: Janie, I have good news. No; great news. Can you and Marty come over to dinner Sunday at six? There'll be chicken Marengo. Bye.

Ring. Beep.

HARRIET: Harriet again. Where are you? If you guys don't show up tomorrow, I'll "hock your china." I miss you.

Dial tone.

OPERATOR: Please hang up. There seems to be a receiver off the hook.

Scene 5

Harriet's apartment. LILLIAN *and* HARRIET *sit with drinks.*

HARRIET: I thought you'd tell me I was insane.

LILLIAN: You're not insane. Impetuous, but not insane. Does Janie like Joe?

HARRIET: Janie's never even met Joe.

LILLIAN: You should talk to her about him. It's important to discuss your life choices with your friends.

HARRIET: Mother, you're so full of homespun advice today.

LILLIAN: I got my hair done yesterday. I read a lot of those women's magazines. You and Joe will have to come over next week for some Jello-O.

Doorbell rings.

JANIE, *offstage:* Harriet, it's me, Janie.

HARRIET *opens the door:* Hi.

JANIE, *with a bouquet of flowers:* These are for you. I was afraid you'd say they're too old. They're too new; they're gold.

HARRIET: No, they're perfect.

JANIE: How are you, Mrs. Cornwall?

LILLIAN: Janie, I'll know you the rest of my life and you'll still call me Mrs. Cornwall. Makes me feel good, baby. The kids in my office call me Lillian and pretend we're colleagues. We're not colleagues. I'm a person of moral and intellectual superiority.

HARRIET: My mother deals from strength.

JANIE: Speaking of strength, guess who called me? Paul Stuart. He said to tell you he really likes you very much and he doesn't understand why you won't return his calls. I'm *awfully* glad he has my number.

LILLIAN: Is this your boss's boss? The one who was so impressed with my potency.

HARRIET: Well, he's my boss now. I was promoted.

HARRIET & JANIE: Yeah!!!! *They hug.*

JANIE: I knew there was good news here. I got the chicken Marengo message and I said something good was happening. I've been trying to call you, but you weren't home, and then I was busy sending the letter B to the Bahamas. "Sesame Street" hired me part-time!

HARRIET & JANIE: Yeah!!!! *They hug again.*

LILLIAN: Perhaps I should feel threatened. I'm surrounded by a generation of achieving younger women.

HARRIET: I don't think Janie's threatening to anyone. That's her gift.

LILLIAN: Well, she's impressive. Where's your nice young man? Harriet said she invited him to dinner tonight. I was looking forward to meeting him.

JANIE: Uh, Marty's busy tonight. There's a testimonial dinner for his father at Szechuan Taste. One day they'll find out which rabbi he's paying off and close down those places.

LILLIAN: Harriet, maybe Marty's father should cater your wedding? It'll be a first for the Carlyle. And we could keep it in the family.

JANIE, *looking from* LILLIAN *to* HARRIET: Excuse me?

HARRIET: Janie, do you remember, at my whiplash party two weeks ago, I told you I was driving up to a planning conference with Joe? He's the headhunter who got me my job at Colgate. He was a year ahead of me at Harvard.

Well, I've been spending a lot of time with him recently.
And yesterday he asked me to marry him.

JANIE: What?

HARRIET *stands up and announces with pride:* I'm going to
marry Joe Stine.

Pause.

LILLIAN: He'll be all right for a first husband. I'm just kidding.
You know I'm thrilled, baby.

JANIE: Congratulations!

HARRIET: I would have told you earlier, but I didn't even
know it was happening. And my time with Joe has been
so intense, I wasn't able to call you.

JANIE: That's wonderful!

LILLIAN: Janie, you and I will have to plan the shower together. Well, I'm off to the Ming Dynasty.

HARRIET: What?

LILLIAN: I'm taking an Oriental Studies class. Not for credit.
Your mother is broadening herself. I'll leave you girls to
your dinner. Harriet, for the sake of your marriage, move
beyond chicken Marengo. Bye-bye, girls. *Exits.*

JANIE: She's in a good mood.

HARRIET: She's been reading *Redbook.* So, what do you
think?

JANIE: It's wonderful. *Mazel tov.*

HARRIET, *going to the kitchen:* I didn't mean to surprise you
like this. I wanted to have you and Marty to dinner. Are
things okay with Marty?

JANIE: Yeah. Fine.

HARRIET: You okay?

JANIE: Harriet, have you thought about living with Joe first?

Better yet, maybe you should have dinner with Joe first?

HARRIET, *exuberant:* I want to marry him! Janie, he's the only person who's even cared about me in a long time. He listens to me. Tasha's right. You and I deserve a little nachos.

JANIE: *Naches.*

HARRIET: Joe makes me feel like I have a family. I never had a family. I had you and Lillian, but I never felt I could have what other women just assumed they would get.

JANIE: I want to know one thing. I want to know why when I asked you about my living with Marty, you told me you didn't respect women who didn't learn to live alone and pay their own rent? And then, the first chance you have to change your life, you grasp it.

HARRIET: What? Marrying Joe is just a chance that came along.

JANIE: I see. You've been waiting for some man to come along and change your life. And all the things you told me about learning to live alone, and women and friendship, that was so much social nonsense. I feel like an idiot! I made choices based on an idea that doesn't exist anymore.

HARRIET: What choices?

JANIE: Never mind.

HARRIET: Janie, when I told you that, I didn't know what it would be like when Paul Stuart would leave at ten and go home to Cathy and I would have to pretend I wasn't hurt. I didn't know what it would be like to have lunch with Lillian and think I'm on my way to watching "The Rockford Files" reruns. Of course you should learn to live alone and pay your own rent, but I didn't realize what it would feel like for me when I became too good at it. Janie, I know how to come home, put on the news, have a glass of wine, read a book, call you. What I don't know is what to do when there's someone who loves me in the house.

JANIE: I could throw this table at you.

HARRIET: Why? Janie, we're too good friends for you to be jealous.

JANIE: I'm not jealous.

HARRIET: Don't blame me for your doubts about Marty.

JANIE: Harriet, I don't blame you for anything. I'm sorry. Right now I just don't like you very much.

HARRIET: Why? Because I'm leaving you? Because I'm getting married?

JANIE: Because our friendship didn't mean very much to you. You bring me the sugar, the bread, and the salt, and you stand there and tell me you never had a family. Harriet, you never really listened to me and you never really told me about yourself. And that's sad.

HARRIET: Janie, I love you. But you want us to stay girls together. I'm not a girl anymore. I'm almost thirty and I'm alone.

JANIE: You lied to me.

HARRIET: I never lied to you. I lied to myself. It doesn't take any strength to be alone, Janie. It's much harder to be with someone else. I want to have children and get on with my life.

JANIE: What do you do? Fall in with every current the tide pulls in? Women should live alone and find out what they can do, put off marriage, establish a vertical career track; so you do that for a while. Then you almost turn thirty and *Time Magazine* announces, "Guess what, girls? It's time to have it all." Jaclyn Smith is married and pregnant and playing Jacqueline Kennedy. Every other person who was analyzing stocks last year is analyzing layettes this year; so you do that. What *are* you doing, Harriet? Who the hell are you? Can't you conceive of some plan, some time-management scheme that you made up for yourself? Can't you take a chance?

HARRIET: I *am* taking a chance. I hardly know this man.

JANIE: You don't have to force yourself into a situation—a marriage—because it's time.

HARRIET: You're just frightened of being with someone, Janie. You're just frightened of making a choice and taking responsibility for it.

JANIE: That sounds romantic.

HARRIET: That's life.

JANIE: Harriet, you're getting married to someone you've been dating for two weeks. I am much more scared of being alone than you are. But I'm not going to turn someone into the answer for me.

HARRIET: Then you'll be alone.

JANIE: Then I'll be alone. *Pauses.* I better go. I have to get up early with the letter B. If they like this, they'll hire me full-time. In charge of consonants.

HARRIET: Give my love to Marty.

JANIE: I can't. I told him I won't move with him to Brooklyn.

HARRIET: So you'll get an apartment in Manhattan.

JANIE *starts crying:* We broke up. I decided not to see him anymore.

HARRIET: Won't you miss him?

JANIE: I missed him today when I saw someone who looks sweet like him walking down the street, and I'll miss him late tonight.

HARRIET: Maybe you should call him.

JANIE: No.

HARRIET: Life is a negotiation.

JANIE: I don't believe I have to believe that.

HARRIET: Janie, it's too painful not to grow up.

JANIE: That's not the way I want to grow up. *Kisses* HARRIET *and starts to go.*

HARRIET: You don't have to separate from me. I'm not leaving you.

JANIE *picks up the trash:* Want me to throw this out for you?

HARRIET: Sure.

JANIE: Do you really think anyone ever met someone throwing out the garbage?

They both shake their heads no. JANIE *exits.*

Scene 6

Janie's apartment. JANIE *is alone, sitting in front of her crates, wrapped in her blanket, holding the swizzle stick that Marty gave her. A romantic version of "Isn't It Romantic" is heard.* JANIE *suddenly begins to cry. The doorbell rings.* JANIE *doesn't answer it.*

SIMON, *offstage:* Janie, Janie.

JANIE, *softly:* What?

Doorbell rings once more.

SIMON: Janie. Janie. It's Dad. Can we come in?

JANIE: Just a second.

TASHA, *offstage:* Janie, the super said he doesn't have the key.

JANIE: I changed the lock.

TASHA: What?

JANIE: Mother, you can't come in until you repeat after me: My daughter is a grown woman.

TASHA: Simon, she's crazy.

JANIE: My daughter is a grown woman.

TASHA: My daughter is a grown woman.

JANIE: This is her apartment.

TASHA: Of course, it's your apartment.

SIMON: For Christ's sake, just tell her . . .

TASHA: This is her apartment.

JANIE: I am to call before I arrive here.

TASHA: I always call. I get the machine.

SIMON: Janie, we can leave this with the doorman.

JANIE: There isn't any doorman here.

TASHA: Simon, maybe she wants to be alone.

JANIE *opens the door:* It's all right, Mother. The six truck drivers just left out the back window.

TASHA *and* SIMON *enter. He carries a box.*

SIMON: Sorry to bother you. We tried calling, but you don't return our calls.

JANIE: I've been busy, Daddy. I'm going on location with the letter C to Canada. They seem to like me.

TASHA: Of course they like you. You're my daughter.

JANIE: I don't think they know *you*, Mother.

TASHA: Simon, give her the package and let's go.

SIMON *puts down the box.*

TASHA: Your father said, "Janie will look like a model in this."

SIMON: You don't have to keep it unless you like it.

JANIE *opens the box. It contains a mink coat.*

SIMON: Do you like it?

TASHA: Give your father a little pleasure. Try it on. *Helps* JANIE *put it on.*

It is very small, a size 4. JANIE *hunches to pull it around herself.*

SIMON: I think it's very nice to your face. The girls are wearing the sleeves short now.

TASHA: I see girls your age wearing theirs to walk the baby carriage.

SIMON: Don't say you like it if you don't like it.

JANIE: I like it. I like it. If I was thirty-six and married to a doctor and a size three, this would be perfect for me.

TASHA: So why aren't you?

JANIE: Do you really want to know why I don't call you? You expect me to dial the phone and say, "Hello, Mother. Hello, Father. Here I am in my mink coat. I just came home from wearing it to walk the carriage. Everything is settled. Everything has worked out wonderfully. Here are your *naches*. Congratulations. I appreciate you."

TASHA: Why do you speak so much Yiddish? We never spoke so much Yiddish around the house.

JANIE: Look, I'm sorry. Things didn't work out as you planned. There's nothing wrong with that life, but it just isn't mine right now.

SIMON: What are you getting so emotional about? Sit. Relax. Look at me. I never get so emotional. Janie, all we did was give you a coat. You'll wear it when its cold. And if you like, you'll wear it when it's hot, like the old ladies in Miami. That's all. No big deal. Are you taking drugs? Your eyes are glassy. Dear, look at her eyes.

TASHA: I don't want to look at her eyes. You know, Janie, I'll never forget when I sent you, as a child, to the Helena Rubenstein Charm School. And you were always late, with your hair in your eyes and your hem hanging down. And Mrs. Rubenstein told me you were an ungrateful child.

JANIE: Mrs. Rubenstein never told you I was an ungrateful child.

TASHA: Simon, what did she tell us?

JANIE: The receptionist at Helena Rubenstein told you I was an ungrateful child. Mother, what do you want from me? You give me a mink coat, and I know you think any other daughter would appreciate this. Helena Rubenstein knows any other daughter would appreciate this. Georgette Klinger's daughter would appreciate this. I am a selfish, spoiled person. Something is the matter with me.

TASHA *gets up:* Something *is* the matter with you. Simon, I have to go dance. I have to work her out of my system.

SIMON: Dear, relax.

JANIE: I don't see how I can help you understand what I'm doing. Neither of you ever lived alone; you never thought maybe I won't have children and what will I do with my life if I don't.

TASHA: All right. You're the smart one. I'm the stupid one. I haven't taught you anything.

JANIE, *furious:* Mother, think about it. Did you teach me to marry a nice Jewish doctor and make chicken for him? You order up breakfast from a Greek coffee shop every morning. Did you teach me to go to law school and wear gray suits at a job that I sort of like every day from nine to eight? You run out of here in leg warmers and tank tops to dancing school. Did you teach me to compromise and lie to the man I live with and say I love you when I wasn't sure? You live with your partner; you walk Dad to work every morning.

TASHA: Now I understand. Everything is my fault. I should have been like the other mothers: forty chickens in the freezer and mah-jongg all afternoon. Janie, I couldn't live like that. God forbid. You think your father would have been happy with one of those women with the blond hair and the diamonds? And I'll tell you something else: you and Ben wouldn't have come out as well as you did. I believe a person should have a little originality—a little "you know." Otherwise you just grow old like everybody else. Let's go, Simon. Honey, you don't have to call us. You don't even have to let us know how you are. You do what you want. *Starts to go.*

JANIE: Wait a minute.

TASHA: I'm a modern woman too, you know. I have my dancing, I have your father, and I have my beautiful grandchild and Ben. I don't need you to fill up my life. I'm an independent woman—a person in my own right. Am I right, Simon?

SIMON: Janie, as for me, what I want is some Sunday before I come over here with a coffee table or a mink coat, you'd call me and say, "Dad, let's get together, I'd like to see you."

TASHA: She doesn't want to see us.

Pause.

JANIE *looks at her parents:* I do want to see you. But you don't have to call every morning to sing "Sunrise—Sunset," and you don't have to bring a mink coat or a coffee table, or even a Russian taxicab driver for me to marry.

SIMON: Whatever happened to him? He was a nice boy.

JANIE: All you have to do is trust me a little bit. I believe a person should have a little originality, a little "you know"; otherwise you just grow old like everybody else. And you know, Janie, I like life, life, life. Mother, sit, relax, let me figure it out.

TASHA: But, honey, if I sit, who's going to dance?

JANIE: Everything presses itself out.

TASHA: Unfortunately, Janie, the clock has a funny habit of keeping on ticking. I want to know who's going to take care of you when we're not around anymore.

JANIE: I guess *I* will. *Takes her mother's hand.* Mother, don't worry. I'm Tasha's daughter. I know; "I am."

TASHA: That's right. "I am."

JANIE *touches Tasha's cheek. They embrace.*

SIMON: And, Janie, from a man's point of view, the next time someone wants you to make him chicken, you tell him I was at your sister-in-law Christ's house the other day and she ordered up lamb chops from the Madison Delicatessen. How hard is it to cook lamb chops? You just stick them in the broiler. If Christ can order up lamb chops— and she's a girl from Nebraska—you don't have to make anybody chicken. Believe me, you were born to order up.

JANIE: Sounds like manifest destiny.

SIMON: In fact, I have the number. We could have a family dinner right now.

TASHA: No, Simon. Let's go home.

SIMON *kisses* JANIE: Good-bye, Janie.

JANIE: Good-bye, Daddy.

TASHA: Good-bye, honey.

JANIE: Mother, one more thing. Take back your mink. *Takes it off and puts it over Tasha's shoulders.*

TASHA: Fits me perfectly.

JANIE: Fits you perfectly.

TASHA: Where's my partner? *Sweeps up to* SIMON, *and, arm in arm, they exit.*

JANIE *takes a deep breath in the silence. She picks up her blanket and folds it neatly, picks up the mink box and sets it on a crate. It's time, finally, to unpack. She lifts blanket, box, and crate and starts to exit into the bedroom. The telephone rings.*

CYNTHIA PETERSON *on phone machine:* Janie, it's Cynthia Peterson. It's my thirty-fourth birthday. I'm alone. Nothing happened with Mr. Houston. I should have married Mark Silverstein in college. Janie, by the time I'm thirty-five, this is what I want.

JANIE *flaps her foot:* Flap.

CYNTHIA PETERSON: I want a hundred thousand dollars a year, a husband, a baby. Janie, are you there? I hear breathing.

JANIE *takes another step:* Flap heel.

CYNTHIA PETERSON: I think someone's there. Whoever you are, there's nothing there worth taking.

JANIE *moves and taps:* Flap, flap, flap, touch. Flap, flap, flap, touch.

CYNTHIA PETERSON: Janie, I met a man at the deli last night. He asked me if I wanted to have a beer in his apartment at one o'clock in the morning. Do you think I should have gone?

JANIE *starts to tap with some assurance as the tape continues.*

CYNTHIA PETERSON: There was an article in the *New York Post* that there are 1,000 men for every 1,123 New York hubby hunters.

Music comes in, "Isn't It Romantic," as JANIE *crosses and picks up a hat and an umbrella.*

CYNTHIA PETERSON: And there was this picture of an eligible man. He's an actor and he likes painting. I like painting. Should I call him?

Music gets louder. JANIE *dances as* CYNTHIA *fades. A spot picks up* JANIE *dancing beautifully, alone.*

CYNTHIA PETERSON: I could take him to the Guggenheim on my membership. How many of these 1,123 women are going to call him? How many are members of the Guggenheim? I don't know if I want to marry an actor. Maybe I should wait for tomorrow's eligible bachelor.

Spot fades on JANIE *twirling with the hat and umbrella.*

END

THE HEIDI
CHRONICLES

To Christopher

The Heidi Chronicles was first produced April 6, 1988, in workshop by The Seattle Repertory Theatre (in association with Playwrights Horizons). It was then presented by Playwrights Horizons in New York City, on December 12, 1988. It was directed by Daniel Sullivan; the sets were designed by Thomas Lynch; costumes by Jennifer von Mayrhauser; lighting by Pat Collins; sound by Scott Lehrer; slides by Wendell Harrington. Roy Harris was production stage manager; Carl Mulert was production manager. The cast was as follows:

HEIDI HOLLAND	*Joan Allen*
SUSAN JOHNSTON	*Ellen Parker*
CHRIS BOXER, MARK, TV ATTENDANT, WAITER, RAY	*Drew McVety*
PETER PATRONE	*Boyd Gaines*
SCOOP ROSENBAUM	*Peter Friedman*
JILL, DEBBIE, LISA	*Anne Lange*
FRAN, MOLLY, BETSY, APRIL	*Joanne Camp*
BECKY, CLARA, DENISE	*Sarah Jessica Parker*

The play moved to the Plymouth Theatre on Broadway, March 9, 1989. It was produced by the Shubert Organization, Suntory International Corp., and James Walsh in association with Playwrights Horizons. The cast remained the same, except that Cynthia Nixon replaced Sarah Jessica Parker as Becky, Clara, and Denise.

CHARACTERS

In order of appearance:
HEIDI HOLLAND
SUSAN JOHNSTON
CHRIS BOXER
PETER PATRONE
SCOOP ROSENBAUM
JILL
FRAN
BECKY GROVES
DEBBIE
CLARA
MARK
MOLLY MC BRIDE
LISA FRIEDLANDER
DENISE
BETSY
TV ATTENDANT
APRIL LAMBERT
WAITER
SANDRA ZUCKER-HALL
RAY

ACT ONE

Prologue: A lecture hall, New York, 1989
Scene 1: Chicago, 1965
Scene 2: Manchester, New Hampshire, 1968
Scene 3: Ann Arbor, Michigan, 1970
Scene 4: Chicago, 1974
Scene 5: New York, 1977

ACT TWO

All scenes take place in New York.

Prologue: A lecture hall, 1989
Scene 1: An apartment, 1980
Scene 2: A TV studio, 1982
Scene 3: A restaurant, 1984
Scene 4: The Plaza Hotel, 1986
Scene 5: A pediatrics ward, 1987
Scene 6: An apartment, 1989

ACT ONE

Prologue

1989. Lecture hall, Columbia University. HEIDI *stands in front of a screen. Slides of paintings are shown as she lectures.*

HEIDI: Sofonisba Anguissola painted this portrait of her sister, Minerva, in 1559. Not only was Sofonisba a painter with an international reputation, but so were her six sisters. Here's half the family in Sofonisba's "Three Sisters Playing Chess," painted in 1555. *Looks up at the painting.* "Hello, girls." Although Sofonisba was praised in the seventeenth century as being a portraitist equal to Titian, and at least thirty of her paintings are known to us, there is no trace of her, or any other woman artist prior to the twentieth century, in your current art history textbook. Of course, in my day this same standard text mentioned no women "from the dawn of history to the present." Are you with me? Okay.

Clara Peeters, roughly 1594 to 1657, whose undated self-portrait we see here, was, I believe, the greatest woman artist of the seventeenth century. And now I'd like you to name ten others. Peeters' work predates the great period of northern still-life painting. In her breakfast paintings—Clara's term, not mine—she used more geometry and less detail than her male peers. Notice here the cylindrical silver canister, the disk of the plate, and the triangular cuts in the cheese. Trust me, this is cheese. After breakfast, in fact, Clara went through a prolonged cheese period.

A leap, but go with me. "We Both Must Fade," painted in 1869 by the American genre painter Lily Martin Spencer, combines in a "vanitas" painting the formal portraiture of Sofonisba and the still-life composition of Peeters. We have a young woman posing in an exquisitely detailed dress, surrounded by symbolic still-life objects. The fading flower and the clockface are both reminders of mortality and time passing, while the precious jewelry spilling out is an allusion to the transcience of earthly possessions. This portrait can be perceived as a meditation on the brevity of youth, beauty, and life. But what can't?

Okay. To the vital issue at hand: how to remember these paintings for next week's midterm. Sofonisba Anguissola, formal portraiture in the style of Titian with a taste for red jewelry; Clara Peeters, still-life master of geometry and cheese. As for Mrs. Lily Martin Spencer and "We Both Must Fade," frankly, this painting has always reminded me of me at one of those horrible high-school dances. And you sort of want to dance, and you sort of want to go home, and you sort of don't know what you want. So you hang around, a fading rose in an exquisitely detailed dress, waiting to see what might happen.

Scene 1

1965. A high-school dance, with folding chairs, streamers, and a table with a punch bowl. Two sixteen-year-old girls enter, SUSAN, wearing a skirt and a cardigan sweater, and HEIDI in a traditional A-line dress. The girls find a corner and look out at the dance floor as they sing and sway to the music. "The Shoop Shoop Song" is playing. "Does he love me? I wanna know. How can I tell if he loves me so."

SUSAN:

    Is it in his eyes?

HEIDI:

    Oh, nooooooo, you'll be deceived.

SUSAN:

    Is it in his eyes?

HEIDI:

    Oh, no, he'll make believe.

SUSAN: Heidi! Heidi! Look at the guy over at the radiator.

HEIDI: Which one?

SUSAN: In the blue jeans, tweed jacket, and the Weejuns.

HEIDI: They're all wearing that.

SUSAN: The one in the vest, blue jeans, tweed jacket, and Weejuns.

HEIDI: Cute.

SUSAN: Looks kinda like Bobby Kennedy.

HEIDI: Kinda. Yup, he's definitely cute.

SUSAN: Look! He can twist and smoke at the same time. I love that! SUSAN *unbuttons her sweater and pulls a necklace out of her purse.*

HEIDI: Susie, what are you doing?

SUSAN: Heidi, men rely on first impressions. Oh, God, he's incredible! Heidi, move!

HEIDI: What, Susie?

SUSAN: Just move! The worst thing you can do is cluster. 'Cause then it looks like you just wanna hang around with your girlfriend. But don't look desperate. Men don't dance with desperate women. Oh my God! There's one coming. Will you start moving! Trust me.

HEIDI *begins to move. She doesn't notice a boy,* CHRIS BOXER, *coming over to her.*

CHRIS: Hi.

HEIDI: Hi.

CHRIS: Hi. I'm Chris Boxer, Student Council president here.

HEIDI: I'm Heidi Holland, editor of the newspaper somewhere else.

CHRIS: Great. I knew I could talk to you. Do you want to dance? *Begins to twist.*

HEIDI: I'm sorry. I can't leave my girlfriend. *Moves back to* SUSAN.

SUSAN: I don't believe this.

HEIDI: This is my girlfriend, Susan Johnston. We came to the dance together.

CHRIS: Oh, I thought you were alone.

SUSAN: She is. We just met.

CHRIS: Well, very nice to meet you both. *Begins to walk away.*

SUSAN: Chris, don't go.

HEIDI: Please don't go. We can all dance together. We can form a line and hully-gully, baby.

CHRIS, *uncomfortable, looks around:* Well, that's the headmaster. I guess I have to go and, uh, ask him how it's going. Keep the faith. *He snaps his fingers.*

HEIDI: We will.

CHRIS *begins to walk away again.*

SUSAN *calls after him:* Nice meeting you. *Begins whispering to* HEIDI. I can't believe you did that. Heidi, we're at a dance! You know, girl meets boy. They hold hands walking in the sand. Then they go to the Chapel of Love. Get it?

HEIDI: Got it.

"Satisfaction" begins to play.

VOICE: The next dance is gonna be a Ladies' Choice.

SUSAN, *thrilled:* All right. Let's get organized here. Heidi, stand in front of me. I can't ask Twist and Smoke to dance with my skirt this long. What should I say to him? SUSAN *rolls up her skirt.*

HEIDI: Ask him how he coordinates the twisting with the smoking.

SUSAN: You know, as your best friend, I must tell you frankly that you're going to get really messed up unless you learn to take men seriously.

HEIDI: Susan, there is absolutely no difference between you and me and him. Except that he can twist and smoke at the same time and we can get out of gym with an excuse called "I have my monthly."

SUSAN: Shit! It's still too long. *Continues to roll the waist of her skirt until it is midthigh.* Can you get home all right by yourself?

HEIDI: He'll never even suspect I even know you.

SUSAN: Wish me luck!

HEIDI *kisses her on the cheek:* Luck!

SUSAN *jumps back in horror:* Heidi! Don't!

HEIDI: Keep the faith! *Snaps her fingers as* CHRIS BOXER *did.*

SUSAN: Shhhhh! Don't make me laugh or my skirt will roll down.

HEIDI: I'll call you tomorrow.

SUSAN *exits as she waves good-bye to* HEIDI. HEIDI *sits on a chair, takes out a book, reads it for a moment, then puts it on her lap as she stares out. "Play with Fire" is played.* PETER, *a young man in a St. Mark's school blazer, approaches. He looks at her. She smiles and looks down.*

PETER: You must be very bright.

HEIDI: Excuse me?

PETER: You look so bored you must be very bright.

HEIDI: I'm sorry?

PETER: Don't be sorry. I appreciate bored people. Bored, depressed, anxious. These are the qualities I look for in a woman. Your lady friend is dancing with the gentleman who looks like Bobby Kennedy. I find men who smoke and twist at the same time so dreary.

HEIDI: Not worth the coordination, really.

PETER: Do you have any?

HEIDI: I can sit and read at the same time.

PETER: What book is that?

HEIDI: *Death Be Not Proud.*

PETER: Of course.

HEIDI: A favorite of mine at dances.

PETER: I was drawn to you from the moment I saw you shielding that unfortunate wench rolling up her garments in the tempest.

HEIDI: I'm sorry.

PETER: Please. Don't apologize for being the most attractive woman on this cruise.

HEIDI: Cruise?

PETER: She docks tonight in Portsmouth. And then farewell to the *Queen Mary*. Forever to harbor in Long Beach, California. *C'est triste, n'est pas?*

HEIDI: *Ce n'est pas bon.*

PETER, *excitedly:* Our tragic paths were meant to cross. I leave tomorrow for the sanatorium in Zurich. *Coughs.*

HEIDI: How odd! I'm going to the sanatorium in Milan. *Coughs. He offers her his handkerchief. She refuses.*

PETER: My parents are heartbroken. They thought I was entering Williams College in the fall.

HEIDI: My parents put down a deposit at Vassar.

PETER: We've only this night together. I'm Peter, a small noise from Winnetka. I tried to pick out your name . . . Amanda, Lady Clara, Estelle . . .

HEIDI: It's . . .

PETER: No, don't tell me. I want to remember you as you are. Beside me in the moonlight, the stars above us . . .

HEIDI: The sea below us.

PETER: Glenn Miller and the orchestra. It's all so peaceful.

HEIDI: Mmmmmm. Quite peaceful.

"The Shoop Shoop Song" is heard again.

PETER: The twist-and-smokers are heaving themselves on their lady friends. This must be the final song. Would you do me the honor of one dance?

HEIDI: Certainly.

PETER: Ahhh! "The Shoop Shoop Song." Baroque but fragile.

HEIDI: Melodic but atonal.

PETER: Will you marry me?

HEIDI: I covet my independence.

PETER: Perhaps when you leave the sanatorium, you'll think otherwise. I want to know you all my life. If we can't marry, let's be great friends.

HEIDI: I will keep your punch cup, as a memento, beside my pillow.

PETER: Well, shall we hully-gully, baby?

HEIDI: Really, I . . .

PETER: Don't worry. I'll teach you.

He begins to do a form of shimmy line dance. Holding Heidi's hand, he instructs her. The dance is somewhat interpretive and becomes a minuet. They sing as they dance together.

PETER:

How 'bout the way he acts?

HEIDI:

Oh, noooo, that's not the way.

PETER:

And you're not listenin' to all I say.
If you wanna know if he loves you so . . .

Takes Heidi's waist and dips her.

PETER:

It's in his kiss.

HEIDI & PETER:

Oh, yeah! It's in his kiss!

They continue to dance as the lights fade.

Scene 2

1968. A dance. There are "Eugene McCarthy for President" signs. "Take a Piece of My Heart," by Janis Joplin and Big Brother and the Holding Company, can be heard. A hippie in a Sergeant Pepper jacket smokes a joint. When HEIDI *enters, he offers her a drag.* HEIDI, *wearing a floral shawl, refuses and stands by the food table.* SCOOP ROSENBAUM, *intense but charismatic, in blue jeans and work shirt, goes over to her. He takes a beer from a bucket on stage.*

SCOOP: Are you guarding the chips?

HEIDI: No.

SCOOP: Then you're being very difficult.

HEIDI: Please, help yourself.

SCOOP: Where are you going?

HEIDI: I'm trying to listen to the music.

SCOOP: Janis Joplin and Big Brother and the Holding Company. A − singer. C+ band. Far less innovative than the Kinks. You know, you really have one hell of an inferiority complex.

HEIDI: I do?

SCOOP: Sure. I have no right to say you're difficult. Don't you believe in human dignity? I mean, you're obviously a liberal, or you wouldn't be here.

HEIDI: I came with a friend.

SCOOP: You came to Manchester, New Hampshire, in a blizzard to ring doorbells for Gene McCarthy because of a friend? Why the fuck didn't you go skiing instead?

HEIDI: I don't ski.

SCOOP *offers* HEIDI *a potato chip:* B— texture. C+ crunch. You go to one of those Seven Sister schools?

HEIDI: How did you know?

SCOOP: You're all concerned citizens.

HEIDI: I told you, I came because of a friend.

SCOOP: That's bullshit. Be real. You're neat and clean for Eugene. You think if you go door to door and ring bells, this sucker will become president, and we'll all be good people, and wars in places you've never heard of before will end, and everyone will have enough to eat and send their daughters to Vassar. Like I said, neat and clean for Eugene.

HEIDI: Would you excuse me?

SCOOP *smiles and extends his hand to her:* It's been lovely chatting with me.

HEIDI: A pleasure.

SCOOP: What's your name?

HEIDI: Susan.

SCOOP: Susan what?

HEIDI: Susan Johnston. See ya.

SCOOP: Hey, Susan Johnston, wouldn't you like to know who I am?

HEIDI: Uh . . .

SCOOP: C'mon. Nice girl like you isn't going to look a man in the eye and tell him, "I have absolutely no interest in you. You've been incredibly obnoxious and your looks are B—."

HEIDI: Why do you grade everything?

SCOOP: I used to be a very good student.

HEIDI: Used to?

SCOOP: I dropped out of Princeton. The Woodrow Wilson School of International Bullshit.

HEIDI: So what do you do now?

SCOOP: This and that. Here and there.

HEIDI: You work for McCarthy? Well, you *are* at a McCarthy dance.

SCOOP: I came with a friend. Susan, don't you know this is just the tip of the iceberg? McCarthy is irrelevant. He's a C+ Adlai Stevenson. The changes in this country could be enormous. Beyond anything your sister mind can imagine.

HEIDI: Are you a real-life radical?

SCOOP: You mean, do I make bombs in my parents' West Hartford basement? Susan, how could I be a radical? I played lacrosse at Exeter and I'm a Jew whose first name is Scoop. You're not very good at nuance. And you're too eager to categorize. I'm a journalist. I'm just here to have a look around.

HEIDI: Do you work for a paper?

SCOOP: Did they teach you at Vassar to ask so many inane questions in order to keep a conversation going?

HEIDI: Well, like I said, I have to go meet my friend.

SCOOP: Me too. I have to meet Paul Newman.

HEIDI: Please tell him Susan says "Hi."

SCOOP: You don't believe I have to meet Paul Newman.

HEIDI: I'm sure you do.

SCOOP: I'm picking him up at the airport and taking him and Mr. McCarthy to a press conference. Paul's a great guy. Why don't you come drinking with us? We can rap over a few brews.

HEIDI: I'm sorry. I can't.

SCOOP: Why not?

HEIDI: I just can't.

SCOOP: Susan, let me get this straight. You would rather drive back to Poughkeepsie with five virgins in a Volkswagen discussing Norman Mailer and birth control on

dangerous frozen roads than go drinking with Eugene
McCarthy, Paul Newman, and Scoop Rosenbaum?
You're cute, Susan. Very cute.

HEIDI: And you are really irritating!

SCOOP: That's the first honest thing you've said all night!
Lady, you better learn to stand up for yourself. I'll let
you in on a scoop from Scoop.

HEIDI: Did they teach you construction like that at Princeton?

SCOOP: I dig you, Susan. I dig you a lot.

HEIDI: Can we say "like" instead of "dig"? I mean, while I
am standing up for myself . . .

SCOOP: I like you, Susan. You're prissy, but I like you a
lot.

HEIDI: Well, I don't know if I like you.

SCOOP: Why should you like me? I'm arrogant and difficult.
But I'm very smart. So you'll put up with me. What?

HEIDI: What what?

SCOOP: You're thinking something.

HEIDI: Actually, I was wondering what mothers teach their
sons that they never bother to tell their daughters.

SCOOP: What do you mean?

HEIDI: I mean, why the fuck are you so confident?

SCOOP: Ten points for Susan!

HEIDI: Have we moved on to points, from letter grades?

SCOOP: There's hope for you. You're going to be quite the
little politico.

HEIDI: I'm planning to be an art historian.

SCOOP: Please don't say that. That's really suburban.

HEIDI: I'm interested in the individual expression of the human soul. Content over form.

SCOOP: But I thought the point of contemporary art is that
the form becomes the content. Look at Albers' "Homage
to a Square." Three superimposed squares, and we're

talking perception, integration, isolation. Just three squares, and they reflect the gross inadequacies of our society. Therefore, your argument is inconclusive.

HEIDI: Don't give me a Marxist interpretation of Albers.

SCOOP: You really are one fuck of a liberal! Next thing you'll tell me is how much Herbert Marcuse means to you. What?

HEIDI: Nothing.

SCOOP: I don't fuckin' believe it! You've never read Marcuse!

HEIDI: Isn't Paul Newman waiting for you, Scoop?

SCOOP: Isn't your friend waiting for you, *Heidi? Jumps up.* Basket, Rosenbaum. Thirty points. The score is 30 to 10.

HEIDI: How did you know my name?

SCOOP: I told you I'm a journalist. Do you really think any-thing—*takes out the paper to show her*—gets by the *Liberated Earth News?*

HEIDI: That's your paper?

SCOOP: Editor in chief. Circulation 362 and growing. Okay. Truth. I know your name is Heidi because it says so right here—*looks in the paper and then up at her breast*—on your name tag. Heidi. H-E-I-D-I.

HEIDI: Oh!

SCOOP: Ohh!

HEIDI: Oh, well . . . *Begins to pull the tag off.*

SCOOP: You don't have to look at the floor.

HEIDI: I'm not.

SCOOP: I've got nothing on you so far. Why are you so afraid to speak up?

HEIDI: I'm not afraid to speak up.

SCOOP: Heidi, you don't understand. You're the one this is all going to affect. You're the one whose life this will all change significantly. Has to. You're a very serious person.

In fact, you're the unfortunate contradiction in terms—a serious good person. And I envy you that.

HEIDI: Thank you. I guess.

SCOOP: Yup. You'll be one of those true believers who didn't understand it was all just a phase. The Trotskyite during Lenin's New Economic Policy. The worshiper of fallen images in Christian Judea.

HEIDI: And you?

SCOOP: Me? I told you. I'm just here to have a look around.

HEIDI: What if you get left behind?

SCOOP: You mean if, after all the politics, you girls decide to go "hog wild," demanding equal pay, equal rights, equal orgasms?

HEIDI: All people deserve to fulfill their potential.

SCOOP: Absolutely.

HEIDI: I mean, why should some well-educated woman waste her life making you and your children tuna-fish sandwiches?

SCOOP: She shouldn't. And, for that matter, neither should a badly educated woman. Heidella, I'm on your side.

HEIDI: Don't call me Heidella. It's diminutive.

SCOOP: You mean "demeaning," and it's not. It's endearing.

HEIDI: You're deliberately eluding my train of thought.

SCOOP: No. I'm subtly asking you to go to bed with me . . . before I go meet Paul Newman.

Pause.

HEIDI: Oh.

SCOOP: You have every right to say no. I can't guarantee absolute equality of experience.

HEIDI: I can take care of myself, thanks.

SCOOP: You've already got the lingo down, kiddo. Pretty soon you'll be burning bras.

HEIDI: Maybe I'll go "hog wild."

SCOOP: I hope so. Are you a virgin?

HEIDI: Excuse me?

SCOOP: If you choose to accept this mission, I'll find out one way or the other.

HEIDI, *embarrassed:* That's okay.

SCOOP: Why do you cover your mouth when you talk about sex?

HEIDI: Hygiene.

SCOOP *takes her hand away from her mouth:* I told you. You're a serious good person. And I'm honored. Maybe you'll think fondly of all this in some Proustian haze when you're thirty-five and picking your daughter up from Ethical Culture School to escort her to cello class before dinner with Dad, the noted psychiatrist and Miró poster collector.

HEIDI: No. I'll be busy torching lingerie.

SCOOP: Maybe I'll remember it one day when I'm thirty-five and watching my son's performance as Johnny Appleseed. Maybe I'll look at my wife, who puts up with me, and flash on when I was editor of a crackpot liberal newspaper and thought I could fall in love with Heidi Holland, the canvassing art historian, that first snowy night in Manchester, New Hampshire, 1968.

HEIDI: Are you guarding the chips?

SCOOP: No. I trust them.

He kisses her passionately as "White Rabbit" begins playing. SCOOP *then looks at his watch and gathers his coat. He begins to leave the room and turns back to* HEIDI. *She looks at her watch and follows him. He clenches his fist in success.*

Scene 3

1970. *Church basement in Ann Arbor, Michigan.* JILL, *forty,
immaculate in a whale turtleneck and a pleated skirt, and*
FRAN, *thirty, in army fatigues, are setting out Danish pastry,
cookies, and coffee. Aretha Franklin's "Respect" blares in the
background.* FRAN *dances and sings along, "Sock it to me,
sock it to me."*

JILL: Fran, I think it would be much cozier if we met next
   time in one of our homes.
FRAN: Jill, we're not the fuckin' Junior League.
JILL: I just hope that everyone is comfortable here. *Begins
   moving chairs.* Maybe we should rearrange things and
   make a conversation nook.
FRAN: You sound like my fuckin' mother. She decorates with
   sheets. *Begins to arrange chairs.*

BECKY, *seventeen, in blue jeans and a poncho, enters while
they are moving chairs and singing.*

FRAN *looks up, notices her:* Hi there.
JILL: Hi.
FRAN: We're just getting into the mood. *Shuts off the music.*
   All right, A-RE-THA!
JILL: Can we help you?
BECKY: Sure. I'm Becky Groves. I saw your poster upstairs.

JILL *and* FRAN *immediately go over to* BECKY *and embrace
her.*

JILL: Becky, I'm Jill and I'm *so* glad you came.

FRAN: Becky, I'm Fran and I'm *so* glad you came.

JILL *takes a plate of cookies over to* BECKY: Becky, how about a peanut-butter granola cookie? We each take turns providing the goodies.

FRAN: "Goodies?" Jill, we're also not the fuckin' Brownies.

BECKY: I sometimes call sweets and cookies "goodies."

JILL: Thank you, Becky.

FRAN: Becky, please let me know if I come on a little strong. I'm trying to work through that.

JILL: I love you, Fran.

HEIDI *and* SUSAN *enter. Both are wearing blue jeans, hiking boots, and down jackets.*

SUSAN: Sorry. Sorry. I'm sorry we're late. Those snowdrifts are mammoth.

FRAN: Bigger than Aphrodite's tits.

FRAN *and* JILL *embrace* SUSAN.

JILL: Hello, Susan. It's *so* good to see you.

FRAN: Hello, Susan. It's *so* good to see you.

SUSAN: This is my friend Heidi. She's visiting for the week.

JILL *embraces* HEIDI: Hello, Heidi. It's *so* good to see you.

FRAN: This is Becky, who is joining us this week.

SUSAN *embraces* BECKY: Hello, Becky. It's *so* good to see you.

FRAN: All right! Let the good times roll!

They all sit down. HEIDI *moves her chair and sits slightly outside the circle, behind* FRAN.

JILL: I'd like to call to order this meeting of the Huron Street Ann Arbor Consciousness-raising Rap Group. Heidi, Becky, since you're new, I want you to know that everything here is very free, very easy. I've been a member of the group for about five months now. I'm a mother of four daughters, and when I first came I was, as Fran would say, "a fuckin' Hostess cupcake." Everybody in my life—my husband, Bill, my daughters, my friends—could lean on perfect Jill. The only problem was, there was one person I had completely forgotten to take care of.

BECKY: Who was that?

JILL: Jill.

BECKY: I feel that way sometimes.

SUSAN: We all feel that way sometimes.

BECKY: You do?

FRAN: No. We grow up on fuckin' "Father Knows Best" and we think we have rights! You think Jane Wyatt demanded clitoral satisfaction from Robert Young? No fuckin' way.

SUSAN: I love you, Fran.

JILL: I love you too, Fran.

FRAN *primps:* Maybe I should dress for combat more often.

SUSAN: Fran, sometimes I think you let your defensiveness overwhelm your tremendous vulnerability.

JILL: Becky, Heidi, you should know that Fran is a gifted physicist, and a lesbian, and we support her choice to sleep with women.

BECKY: Sure.

FRAN: Do you support my choice, Heidi?

HEIDI: I'm just visiting.

FRAN: I have to say right now that I don't feel comfortable with a "just visiting" in the room. I need to be able to come here and reach out to you as my sisters. Okay, Heidi-ho?

HEIDI: Okay.

FRAN: Just don't judge us. Christ, we spend our lives having men judge us. All right, let the good times roll!

SUSAN: I'll start. This week I think I made a little headway, but I'm also afraid I fell back a few paces.

JILL: What did you decide to do about the *Law Review*?

SUSAN: I accepted the position.

JILL: Good.

SUSAN: Becky, I was seriously considering beginning a law journal devoted solely to women's legal issues. But after some pretty heavy deliberation, I've decided to work within the male-establishment power base to change the system. *Gives a power salute.*

JILL: Susan, I'm so proud of you for making a choice.

SUSAN: Do you know my mother would have married me because I have this position?

FRAN: What are you bullshitting about? You're going to work from "within the male-establishment power base." And I'm going to date fuckin' Tricia Nixon. Susan, either you shave your legs or you don't.

SUSAN: I love you, Fran.

FRAN: I scare the shit out of you, Susan.

BECKY: Why are you yelling at her?

SUSAN: Becky, Fran is one of the most honest people I've ever met. She's a great friend.

BECKY: Well, she sounds kinda like Bobby.

JILL: Who's Bobby?

BECKY: Well, Bobby's my boyfriend. Well, we kinda live together. Well, my father and mother split up last year. My father is in the film department here, and last year he made this documentary called *Flower Children of Ypsilanti*. It won a whole bunch of awards and stuff.

HEIDI: Is your father Ed Groves? That's a great documentary.

BECKY: You saw it?

HEIDI: I'm a graduate student. That means I go to a lot of movies.

BECKY: Well, remember that blonde girl with all the rope bracelets who wanted to go to San Francisco so she could sleep with Donovan? She's my father's other wife.

FRAN: Fuckin' mellow yellow.

SUSAN: That's illegal.

BECKY: They're not really married. She just kinda wears his ring. Anyway, when he left, my mom flipped out. So she went to Esalen in California. I think she's talking to a tree or something. She was only going for a week, but it's been six months. So I asked Bobby to move in, at least until I finished high school, but it's kinda not working. But I don't know.

JILL: You don't know what?

BECKY: I mean, I try to be super nice to him. I make all his meals, and I never disagree with him. But then he just gets angry or stoned. So when I need to think things through, I lock the bathroom door and cry. But I try not to make any sound. Now you're all going to hate me, right?

FRAN *goes over to* BECKY: Lamb, no one here is ever going to hate you.

JILL: Becky, do you want to stay with me and my family for a while?

FRAN: I love you, Jill.

SUSAN: I love you, Jill.

BECKY: But I thought you had to learn to take care of Jill.

JILL: Women like us have to learn to give to those who appreciate it, instead of to those who expect it.

FRAN: And those cocksucker assholes have been expecting it for centuries.

BECKY: I think you're all fantastic. You are the best women I have ever met. I am *so* glad I came. *Embraces them all.*

FRAN: Thank you, Becky. All—right! Now I would like to hear from our "visitor" what she thinks of our rap group so far.

HEIDI: I thought you don't want to be judged.

FRAN: I'm asking you to share. Not to judge.

HEIDI: I think Jill is very generous and I think the girl with the rope bracelets would have been much happier with Donovan.

JILL *laughs:* Heidi, where do you go to school?

HEIDI: New Haven.

FRAN: Becky, "New Haven" means "Yale" in Eastern egalitarian circles.

HEIDI: I'm in the Art History Graduate Program. My interest is in images of women from the Renaissance Madonna to the present.

FRAN: A feminist interpretation?

HEIDI: Humanist.

FRAN: Heidi, either you shave your legs or you don't.

HEIDI: I'm afraid I think body hair is in the realm of the personal.

FRAN: What *is* your problem, woman?

HEIDI: I don't really want to share that with you. I'm stingy that way.

SUSAN: My friend Heidi is obsessed with an asshole.

HEIDI: Susie, that's personal.

JILL: "Personal" has kept us apart for so many years. "Personal" means I know what I'm doing is wrong, but I have so little faith in myself, I'm going to keep it a secret and go right on doing it.

BECKY: Heidi, can I rub your back? Sometimes that helps my mother.

JILL: We shouldn't force her. Maybe Heidi isn't at the same place we are.

HEIDI: I *am* at the same place you are.

FRAN: How are you at the same place we are?

HEIDI: I think all people deserve to fulfill their potential.

FRAN: Yeah. Except for you.

HEIDI: What?

FRAN: Heidi, every woman in this room has been taught that the desires and dreams of her husband, her son, or her boss are much more important than her own. And the only way to turn that around is for us, right here, to try to make what *we* want, what *we* desire to be, as vital as it would undoubtedly be to any man. And then we can go out there and really make a difference!

SUSAN: I'm so happy I'm living at this time.

FRAN: Heidi, nothing's going to change until we really start talking to each other.

HEIDI *looks at all of them and sits down. She grabs Susan's hand:* Okay, Fran. I met a guy three years ago at a Eugene McCarthy mixer.

FRAN: Jesus. "Neat and clean for Eugene."

HEIDI: Anyway, we've been seeing each other off and on ever since. He dates a lot of other women, and, uh, I get to see him maybe once every few weeks. He's a teaching fellow at the law school. *Catches herself.* Becky, "the law school" means "Yale Law School." I'm an Eastern egalitarian asshole from Chicago.

JILL: So, big deal.

HEIDI: Thanks.

SUSAN: The point is that Heidi will drop anything—work, a date, even a chance to see me—just to be around this creep.

HEIDI: He is a creep. But he's a charismatic creep.

FRAN: I fuckin' hate charisma.

HEIDI: When I need him, he's aloof. But if I decide to get better and leave him, he's unbelievably attentive.

BECKY: Your asshole sounds just like my asshole.

HEIDI: But you see, Becky, the problem isn't really him. The problem is me. I could make a better choice. I have an old friend, Peter, who I know would be a much better choice. But I keep allowing this guy to account for so much of what I think of myself. I allow him to make me feel valuable. And the bottom line is, I know that's wrong. I would tell any friend of mine that's wrong. You either shave your legs or you don't.

FRAN: I like your friend, Susan. She has a way to go, but she's one smart repressed lady.

HEIDI: Becky, I hope our daughters never feel like us. I hope all our daughters feel so fucking worthwhile. Do you promise we can accomplish that much, Fran? Huh? Do you promise? Do you promise?

FRAN *gets up and embraces* HEIDI: I take it back. I love you, Heidi.

JILL: I love you, Heidi.

BECKY: I love you, Heidi.

SUSAN: This really has a feeling of completion for me. Full circle. Heidi and I grew up together. We were *girl*friends. But I wanted her to be able to meet my *women* friends, because you are all *so* important to me. And, Becky, that includes you. You are very important to me now. *They are all embracing.*

JILL: I think we're all just terrific! And I swear that neither snow nor sleet nor Aphrodite's tits could keep me from getting my ass here.

FRAN *slaps Jill's hands:* All—right, Jill!

BECKY *slaps Jill's hands:* All—right, Jill!

HEIDI & SUSAN *slap Jill's hands:* All—right, Jill!

JILL: All—right, Heidi!

BECKY: All—right, Heidi!

FRAN: All—right, Heidi! *Turns to slap Jill's hand again.* All—right, Jill!

JILL *moves away and changes the subject:* Why don't we all sing a favorite camp song of mine and of my children. Okay? Okay. We all get into a circle and join hands. And it goes like this . . .

They take hands.

JILL, *instructing:*

    Friends, friends, friends,
    We will always be . . .

They repeat the refrain and begin awkwardly to sway.

ALL:

    Friends, friends, friends,
    We will always be . . .

JILL:

    Whether in hail or in dark stormy weather

ALL:

    Whether in hail or in dark stormy weather

JILL:

    Camp Truckahoe will keep us together!

ALL:

    Camp Truckahoe will . . .

FRAN *breaks out of the circle:* Fuck this shit! *Puts Aretha back on.*

ALL *sing along, dancing:*
>R-E-S-P-E-C-T,
>Find out what it means to me.
>Sock it to me, a little respect,

FRAN *leads the women in making a power salute on "a little respect" each time it is sung.*

>Sock it to me, a little respect,.

Scene ends with their arms up and the women proclaiming—

ALL: A little respect!

Scene 4

1974. Outside the Chicago Art Institute. It is raining. Two young women enter with umbrellas and a picket sign: "Chicago Women's Art Coalition." HEIDI *is speaking with a bullhorn.* DEBBIE, *standing beside her, is chic and extremely severe in black. They all chant, "Women in Art!" in front of a banner for an "Age of Napoleon" exhibition.*

HEIDI: This museum is publicly funded by our tax dollars. "Our" means both men and women. The weekly attendance at this institution is sixty percent female. The painting and appreciation classes are seventy percent female. Yet this "great" cultural center recognizes and displays only two female artists. And its current offering, "The Age of Napoleon," includes not one female artist. *Turns to* DEBBIE. No one's stopping.

DEBBIE *takes the bullhorn:* Women artists excluded from this exhibition are Elisabeth Vigée-Lebrun, 1755 to 1842, painter of over 660 portraits; Marie Benoist, 1768 to 1826 . . .

PETER *enters, in jeans. He carries an umbrella, and a backpack. He raises his fist as he chants, interrupting Debbie's speech.*

PETER: No more more master penises! No more master penises! No more master penises!

HEIDI: Peter!

DEBBIE: At two o'clock this afternoon, my sisters and I plan to march on the curator's office and demand equal representation for our vision. We urge you to join us.

PETER *applauds:* That was terrific. Just great! *Extends his hand to* DEBBIE. Hello, Peter Patrone.

DEBBIE *ignores his hand:* Heidi, I'm afraid some of our group may have gone to the wrong location. Clara and I will go have a look around.

PETER: Right. And I'll beat up any beast who dares go in there with a Rembrandt or a Rubens.

DEBBIE *and the two other women walk off.*

HEIDI: Peter, this is *serious!*

PETER: Serious? This is *urgent!* There I was in my lonely intern's cell, reminiscing about the three hundred stab wounds I had stitched last night and contemplating taking two Quaaludes for my slight sore throat, when who should be on the pay phone, to say she can't see me because she'll only be in Chicago for four hours, but my

innocent youth, my lost love, the lovely and talented Miss
Heidi Holland.

HEIDI: Thank you for coming. I think.

PETER: You think? *Looks around.* I'm the only one who came!

HEIDI *kisses him:* You're a good friend.

PETER: *And* I'm a committed and selfless friend! Do you know
what we're missing by being out here? Do you realize
that after today we won't have Dick Nixon to kick around
anymore? Bye-bye Ehrlichperson and Haldeperson.

HEIDI *looks at him.*

PETER: I'm using nonsexist terminology in honor of your
occasion here. *Closes his umbrella.* Looks like the gods
are smiling on "Women in Art." They want to see more
Grandma Moses.

HEIDI: Maybe they want to see more Florine Stettheimer.

PETER: I doubt the gods are that esoteric. *Pauses.* You look
good.

HEIDI: I do?

PETER: A little puffy. A little rhino skin. But you look good.
So are you going to stand here until more women buy
paints and finish a few masterpieces for this sexist, chau-
vinistic, creepo institution to exhibit?

HEIDI: You heard Debbie. We're marching on the curator's
office.

PETER: Debbie? Her name is Debbie? Anyone who wears that
much black and silver is not a Debbie! Surely she's a
Deborah. Heidi, you should change your name to Hei-
darine or Heidigwyth. Then people would take you seriously. They'd be flocking here. Not since Woodstock
Nation!

HEIDI: You've become cruel in my absence.

PETER: Not cruel. Dyspeptic. I've developed a violent narcissistic personality disorder.

HEIDI: You have?

PETER: Don't worry, my darling. According to my mental-health friends, we're heading into a decade of self-obsession. I'm simply at the forefront of the movement. And speaking of the self-obsessed and satisfied, how is Poopsie?

HEIDI: Scoop. He's in Washington, clerking for the Supreme Court.

PETER: Really! He isn't running for president yet! His parents must be ashamed of him. "Harry, Scoop is dead in this house. Do you hear me? Dead!"

HEIDI: Actually, he and my friend Susan were clerking for the same judge.

PETER: So you're still in touch with him.

HEIDI: But I'm not involved with him anymore. I just like sleeping with him.

PETER: What a perky seventies kind of gal you are! You can separate sexual needs from emotional dependencies. Heidi, if you tell me you secrete endorphins when you run, I'm going straight into the curator's office and demand an all-armor retrospective.

HEIDI: Don't bother. They're already planning that. Are you okay?

PETER: Actually, I'm afraid I'm feeling sort of distant from you.

HEIDI: Peter, I was writing my dissertation.

PETER: I'm not criticizing you. It's just how I'm feeling. I haven't seen you in eight months.

HEIDI *takes him over to sit with her on a nearby bench:* Peter, you need a girlfriend. I have got to find you a girlfriend.

PETER: Please don't.

HEIDI: You've never liked my girlfriends.

PETER: *Women* friends, and I like Fran, the furry physicist from Ann Arbor.

HEIDI: Fran is unavailable. I promise I'll find someone.

PETER, *earnestly:* Heidi, I don't play on your team.

HEIDI: So what? Susan says no man really plays on our team. And no man isn't threatened by our potential. Trust me, you're a lot more secure than most.

PETER: Is Susan the one who used to roll up her skirts with straight pins? She was always giving herself stigmatas in the waist.

HEIDI: She's become a radical-shepherdess-counselor.

PETER: Good for her. I've become a liberal-homosexual-pediatrician.

HEIDI: Well, what I mean is, she lives on a Women's Health and Legal Collective in Montana. Susan was clerking for the Supreme Court with Scoop, but, uh, uh, she realized she prefers, uh, uh . . .

PETER: Sheep. She realized she prefers sheep. Makes sense. And I prefer Stanley.

HEIDI: Who?

PETER: My friend's name is Stanley Zinc. He's a child psychiatrist from Johns Hopkins. But he's thinking of quitting in order to study with Merce Cunningham. The sad thing is that Stanley is too old to join the company, and Miss Merce isn't getting any younger either. Anyway, I'm thinking of replacing him with a waiter I met last week. We share a mutual distrust of Laura Nyro. I would have told you all this earlier, but I thought we deserved something more intimate than a phone call. So I chose the Chicago Art Institute.

HEIDI: I wish Debbie would get back.

PETER: Why in God's name would you wish that Debbie would get back?

HEIDI: Because you're being impossible.

PETER: How am I being impossible?

HEIDI: You're being impossible about Susan and her political ideals!

PETER: But I want to celebrate Susan's political ideals!

HEIDI: Fuck off, Peter! *Moves away from him.*

PETER, *with intensity:* Heidi, I'm gay. Okay? I sleep with Stanley Zinc, M.D. And *my* liberation, *my* pursuit of happiness, and the pursuit of happiness of other men like me is just as politically and socially valid as hanging a couple of goddamn paintings because they were signed by someone named Nancy, Gladys, or Gilda. And that is why I came to see you today. I am demanding your equal time and consideration.

WOMEN *from offstage:* Women in Art! Women in Art!

DEBBIE: Heidi!

PETER: Well thank God, Debbie's back and we've got her!

DEBBIE *walks up to* HEIDI *and* PETER. CLARA *stands behind them.*

DEBBIE: I think it's time we made our move. *Takes the bullhorn.* The coalition for Women's Art will be marching on the curator's office. Please join us. Women in Art! *Begins to march.* CLARA *and* HEIDI *follow and chant with her:* Women in Art!

PETER *picks up the picket sign and begins to march with them:* Women in Art!

DEBBIE *stops and turns to* PETER: I find your ironic tone both paternal and caustic. I'm sorry. I can't permit you to join us. This is a women's march.

HEIDI: But I thought our point was that this is *our* cultural institution. "Our" meaning everybody's. Men and women. Him included.

DEBBIE: Heidi, you know this is a women's march.

PETER: Heidi, you march and I'll wait for you here.

HEIDI, *to* DEBBIE: I'm sorry, I can't leave my friend.

DEBBIE: God, I despise manipulative men.

PETER: Me too.

DEBBIE: Suit yourself, Heidi. *Gets on the bullhorn again.* Women in Art! *Marches off.*

PETER: It's too bad she didn't let me march. I know the curator.

HEIDI: Really? What team does he play on?

PETER: Guess.

HEIDI: Oh, Christ.

PETER: Heidi, I know somewhere you think my world view is small and personal and that yours resonates for generations to come.

HEIDI: I'm going to hit you.

PETER: I dare you. C'mon, put up your dukes. *Takes her hand and punches it against his arm.* That's for my having distorted sexual politics.

HEIDI: Correct.

PETER *punches himself with her hand again:* And that's because your liberation is better than mine.

HEIDI: Correct again.

PETER *punches himself with her hand again:* And that's for my decision to treat sick children rather than shepherd radical sheep. *Hits himself.* And that's for being paternal. And caustic.

HEIDI: Correct. *Begins hitting him on her own.* And that's for being so goddamn . . .

PETER: Narcissistic? Supercilious?

HEIDI: No. Um . . .

PETER: Sounds like . . .

HEIDI: Oh, I give up. *Suddenly hits him again.* And that's for liking to sleep with men more than women. *Hits him again.* And that's for not being desperately and hopelessly in love with me.

PETER: That hurts!

HEIDI: Suffer.

PETER *hits her:* And that's for making me feel guilty.

HEIDI: I did?

PETER: Yes.

HEIDI *sighs as if it's all over.*

PETER *hits her again:* And that's for not remembering our tenth anniversary.

HEIDI: We've known each other for ten years?

PETER: Well, nine, but we don't look it. *Puts his arm around her.* Heidi, for the first time in my life, I'm optimistic. We just might have very happy lives, with enough women's art for everybody. Judy Chicago in the morning, Judy Chicago in the evening, Judy Chicago at dinnertime. Just don't lose your sense of humor or marry that Poop.

HEIDI: Scoop. *Pauses as she looks at him.* Peter, I'd like to meet Stanley Zinc, doctor-dancer.

They embrace. But PETER *pulls away as he looks out.*

PETER: But not imminently, I hope. I left out one thing. Heidi, I invited the waiter to meet me here for lunch today, and— take a deep breath—he's actually shown up.

HEIDI, *looking out:* He's cute.

PETER: He's adorable.

HEIDI: He's okay.

MARK *comes up to them:* Hi.

PETER: Hi. Mark, this is Heidi.

MARK: Hi.

HEIDI: Hi.

PETER: Heidi, Mark. So, what happened?

MARK: It was sad in a way. He was sweating and everything.
I wonder if I'll ever want something as much as he wanted
to be president.

PETER: Sure you will.

MARK: What?

PETER: Me. You'll want me. *Embraces* MARK. HEIDI *tries to
look away.* Everything went great here. I antagonized
Debbie and the entire Women in Art delegation, and sub-
sequently Heidi inflicted me with brutal beatings.

MARK: Really?

HEIDI: It's true. But, Mark, you can make it up to me.

MARK: I can?

HEIDI: We can still march on the curator's office.

PETER: But what about Debbie? This is a women's march.

HEIDI: Mark, I am demanding your equal time and consideration. *Hands him a picket sign.* Women in Art!

HEIDI & MARK: Women in Art! Women in Art!

HEIDI, PETER & MARK *chant together as they link arms and
exit:* Women in Art!

Scene 5

*1977. Anteroom to Pierre Hotel ballroom. The room is empty
except for a few chairs and a table with flowers and a tray
of champagne.* SUSAN *and* MOLLY, *an attractive twenty-six-*

*year-old woman, enter. The dance music, a horah, from the
party next door can be heard.*

MOLLY: Susan, who are those people?

SUSAN: Well, Molly, Heidi's my oldest friend, Peter's a doctor,
the bride I've never met before, and the groom is a prick.

MOLLY: Susie, I have a feeling we're not in Montana anymore.

PETER *and* HEIDI *enter.*

PETER: "Do you, Scoop Rosenbaum, take Lisa Friedlander to
be your bride?" "Well, I feel ambivalent about her. But
I am blocked emotionally, and she went to good schools,
comes from a very good family, and is not particularly
threatening. So, yeah, I do. Anyway, it's time for me to
get married." "And do you, Lisa, take Scoop?" *Speaks
her answer with Lisa's Southern accent.* "Rabbi, ever
since I was a little girl I've been wanting to matriculate
with an M.R.S. degree. I idolize Scoop because he is as
brilliant and will be as rich as my daddy, whom I also
idolize. And I am a slight masochist. Although I do come
from the best Jewish family in Memphis. So, yes, Rabbi,
I do take Scoop." "And now under the eyes of God and
the Pierre Hotel, I pronounce you man and M.R.S.
degree."

SUSAN: I never knew the deity and the Pierre had a package
deal.

PETER: Oh, sure. And for a $10,000 donation, the Holy-Be-
He will throw in table flowers and a four-piece combo.
Honestly, I've never seen a less romantic-looking bride.

HEIDI: Peter, shhh. She looked very tasteful.

PETER: She looked like Woody Woodpecker.

SUSAN: And those bridesmaids looked like flying buttresses!

MOLLY, *giggling:* I'm sure she's a very nice person.

PETER: You're right, Molly. I'm sure she's a very nice person too.

SUSAN: I'm surprised he married someone so bland.

PETER: Susan, do your sisters know you are capable of calling another woman bland!

HEIDI: We should go in there and shake hands.

SUSAN: What is with you today?

HEIDI: I'd marry her.

MOLLY: She had no meat on her.

PETER: I love you, Molly.

HEIDI: They'll be very happy. She's perfect for Scoop.

SCOOP *enters.*

SCOOP: How do you know?

MOLLY: Are you the groom?

SCOOP: Yes.

MOLLY *goes up to* SCOOP: I heard you're a prick.

SUSAN *waves:* Hi, Scoop.

SCOOP *waves:* Hi, Susan.

SUSAN: Scoop, this is my friend Molly McBride, from the Montana Women's Health and Legal Collective.

SCOOP *shakes her hand:* Any sister shepherdess is always a pleasure. *To* PETER: And you must be the pediatrician.

PETER *shakes Scoop's hand: Mazel tov.*

SCOOP: Heidella speaks so fondly of you. I can't understand why she never introduced us.

PETER: Heidella, why have you kept us apart?

HEIDI *glowers at* PETER.

SCOOP: I wish you would all go in to the reception. You're the most interesting people here.

HEIDI: I thought Jonas Salk was here.

MOLLY: I thought Bert Lance was here.

PETER: I thought David Cassidy was here.

SCOOP: They're all here. I told you you're the most interesting people at this party. Please help me out. Without you, I'm just another junior associate at Sullivan Cromwell at another Pierre wedding. It's beyond depressing.

MOLLY: Well, heck, I'll go in. I always like a good party.

SCOOP *puts his arm around* MOLLY: Molly, I think our country is fortunate that Felix Frankfurter didn't meet such an appealing alternative life-style during his formative days. You know I clerked with Susan. She could have been brilliant.

HEIDI: Susan is brilliant.

SCOOP: Brilliance is irrelevant in Montana.

PETER *gets up:* Well, I think our continued presence here is up to Heidi.

SUSAN: Heidi's not saying anything. That means she wants to stay. *Grabs* MOLLY. C'mon, Mol, we're gonna horah like nobody's ever horahed. Maybe we can convince the bride to dump him and become irrelevant in Montana.

SUSAN *and* MOLLY *exit.*

HEIDI: Susan's angry with me.

SCOOP: Susan's crazy.

HEIDI: No she's not.

SCOOP: She's a fanatic and she's crazy. Do you know she was voted one of the ten most attractive "new" women in Washington? I could have been interested in Susan.

PETER: Does Susan know this? She might drown Molly.

HEIDI: Susan's not involved with Molly.

SCOOP: You mean she's like our president? Only in her heart she lusts for other women?

HEIDI: Susan is very committed. She's thinking of going to business school so the collective can become self-sufficient.

SCOOP: She'll be on Wall Street in two years. Believe me.

PETER *is staring at* SCOOP. SCOOP *looks at him.*

PETER: Are you in love?

SCOOP: Excuse me?

PETER: I like to think that when two people our age get married, they are in love.

HEIDI *takes Peter's arm:* Peter's very romantic.

SCOOP: I see. Are you an item now?

HEIDI: No.
PETER, *louder:* Yes.

SCOOP: Makes sense. Lisa marries a nice Jewish lawyer; Heidi marries a warm Italian pediatrician. It's all interchangeable, isn't it? To answer your question am I in love, sure, why not?

HEIDI *squeezes Peter's hand:* Why not?

LISA, *deliberately classy, enters. She speaks with a very slight Southern accent.*

LISA: Sweetie, they're about to play our first dance.

SCOOP: Sweetie, this is Peter Patrone, and his fiancée, Heidi. Peter is a pediatric resident at Bellevue.

LISA: Hey there. How nice to see you.

SCOOP: I was just telling Peter that we're hoping for a large family.

PETER: Not common these days.

LISA: I've always known I wanted to be a mom. I guess that's pretty embarrassing.

PETER, *to* HEIDI: Sweetie, do you think that's embarrassing?

HEIDI: No, sweetie, of course not. Not at all.

LISA: Well, I *am* going to keep up my illustration work.

SCOOP: Lisa's books are very popular.

PETER: Wait a second. Are you Lisa Friedlander the illustrator of *King Ginger, the Lion*?

LISA: You know *King Ginger*?

PETER: The best medical text in this country is *King Ginger Goes to the Hospital*.

SCOOP *puts his arm around* LISA: She's terrific. Isn't she?

PETER: There'll be a riot in my waiting room if you stop working.

SCOOP: Well, we'll see.

LISA: Sweetie, don't be such a little piggie. Dr. Patrone, would you join me for my first dance? Obviously, my husband has decided to be antisocial at his own wedding.

SCOOP: I'm being what?

LISA: Heidi, don't you hate that we can only get a reaction out of our men when they feel competitive? But maybe that's why it's so much fun to push them around. *Winks at* HEIDI *and turns back to* SCOOP. Oh, sweetie, one more thing. There are two women I don't recognize waltzing around the dance floor together. Aunt Florence thinks they might be interlopers. *Takes Peter's arm.* Shake your booties, Doctor.

They exit.

PETER *turns back:* See ya.

HEIDI: Did she just say "Shake your booties, Doctor"?

SCOOP *sits down and sighs in mock despair:* Oh, God, I'm so unhappy!

HEIDI: She must be very talented.

SCOOP: Why did you let me do this?

HEIDI: Me! What do you mean why did *I* let you? I had nothing to do with this.

SCOOP: Yes, you did. Are you marrying this doctor?

HEIDI: Maybe.

SCOOP: Seems like a nice-enough guy.

HEIDI: He's a wonderful guy. He's also gay. Anyway, I'm seeing someone. Sort of living with someone.

SCOOP: So vhere is he? I vant to have a look.

HEIDI: I didn't vant you to meet him. I didn't vant you to have a look.

SCOOP: Is he quality goods?

HEIDI: He's an editor.

SCOOP: An editor?

HEIDI: I met him through work. I'm writing a book of essays.

SCOOP: Academic?

HEIDI: Sort of.

SCOOP: Art history?

HEIDI: Sort of.

SCOOP: Sounds like there's miniseries potential here.

HEIDI: It's called *And the Light Floods in from the Left and Other Overcommitments.* Essays on art and women.

SCOOP *smiles:* Sort of Marcusian.

HEIDI, *increasingly nervous, begins shredding a cocktail napkin:* Well, actually, it's sort of humorous. Well, sort of social observation. I mean, it's sort of a point of view.

SCOOP *takes her hand:* Heidella, don't shred the napkin.

HEIDI: I'm sorry.

SCOOP: Aunt Florence will never recover from who's been at the Pierre today.

HEIDI *bends down and starts picking up the shredded napkin.*

SCOOP: I didn't ask you to clean the room. I just told you not to shred. Maybe you should spend some time on that collective in Montana. Liberate yourself. So, who's this editor?

HEIDI: I don't have to answer these questions.

SCOOP: Heidi, I'm a lawyer and I'm about to become a journalist again. So, yes, actually it'll be easier if you do answer these questions.

HEIDI: What do you mean you're about to become a journalist again?

SCOOP: I'm starting a magazine.

HEIDI: What magazine?

SCOOP: I answered your question, now you have to answer mine. Who's this editor?

HEIDI: Christ . . .

SCOOP: I'm just trying to have a friendly conversation. I'm concerned about you. I care about you. Where did he go to school?

HEIDI: Trinity.

SCOOP: Trinity? Trinity what? Trinity, Cambridge? Trinity, Hartford? Trinity, the lower school?

HEIDI: Trinity, Hartford.

SCOOP, *aghast:* You're sort of living with an editor who went to Trinity College, Hartford!

HEIDI: You've certainly come a long way from the *Liberated Earth News.*

SCOOP: Did I say anything? I didn't say anything. Where does he edit?

HEIDI: *Hustler.*

SCOOP: He should only be half as creative as an editor at *Hustler* and an eighth as well endowed.

HEIDI: You don't even know him.

SCOOP: Yes, I do. Where does he edit? Knopf?

HEIDI: Do you interrogate Lisa like this?

SCOOP: No. I know who Lisa sort of lives with. Simon and Schuster?

HEIDI: No.

SCOOP: Harper and Row?

HEIDI: I don't know.

SCOOP *jumps up as if scoring a basket:* Harper and Row. It's Harper and Row. Way to go, Rosenbaum.

HEIDI: I hate this. I really hate this.

SCOOP: No, you don't. Or you wouldn't have come.

HEIDI: Peter wanted to meet you. That's why we came. He said if I witnessed your ritual, it would put an end to an era. And Susan—for some insane reason, Susan wanted to come too.

SCOOP: Maybe she's got a thing for Bert Lance.

HEIDI: No. Molly wanted to see New York. This all is irrelevant. I'm thinking of writing my book in England. I applied for a Fulbright.

SCOOP, *surprised:* Heidella, if you haven't won this particular round, it doesn't mean you have to drop completely out of the match.

HEIDI: You still use lousy construction.

SCOOP: Yes, I do. And that's what makes me so much more interesting than the editor.

HEIDI: Fuck you.

SCOOP: You still use foul language.

HEIDI: You don't?

SCOOP: My wife doesn't care for it.

HEIDI: Well, clearly she's quality goods.

Pause.

SCOOP: You really don't understand, do you?

HEIDI: I think I do.

SCOOP: No, you don't. But I can explain. Let's say we married and I asked you to devote the, say, next ten years of your life to me. To making me a home and a family and a life so secure that I could with some confidence go out into the world each day and attempt to get an A. You'd say, "No." You'd say, "Why can't we be partners? Why can't we both go out into the world and get an A?" And you'd be absolutely valid and correct.

HEIDI: But Lisa . . .

SCOOP: Do I love her, as your nice friend asked me? She's the best that I can do. Is she an A+ like you? No. But I don't want to come home to an A+. A– maybe, but not A+.

HEIDI: Scoop, we're out of school. We're in life. You don't have to grade everything.

SCOOP: I'm sorry, Heidella. But I couldn't dangle you anymore. And that's why I got married today. So.

HEIDI: So. So now it's all my fault.

SCOOP: Sure it is. You want other things in life than I do.

HEIDI: Really? Like what?

SCOOP: Self-fulfillment. Self-determination. Self-exaggeration.

HEIDI: That's exactly what you want.

SCOOP: Right. Then you'd be competing with me.

Pause.

HEIDI, *softly:* Scoop . . .

SCOOP: What?

HEIDI: Forget it.

SCOOP *puts his arm around her tenderly:* What, baby?

HEIDI: I . . .

SCOOP: It's either/or.

HEIDI: That *is* simply not true!

SCOOP: You don't like the grades. Fuck the grades. Let's try numbers.

HEIDI: I thought you don't use foul language.

SCOOP: I don't. Unless it's helpful. On a scale from one to ten, if you aim for six and get six, everything will work out nicely. But if you aim for ten in all things and get six, you're going to be very disappointed. And, unfortunately, that's why you "quality time" girls are going to be one generation of disappointed women. Interesting, exemplary, even sexy, but basically unhappy. The ones who open doors usually are.

HEIDI: But you're willing to settle for a secure six?

SCOOP: I've got more important things to worry about.

HEIDI: Your magazine?

SCOOP: Just things. It's all home cooking in the crock pot you bought us. By the way, I was hurt by that. It's not a very personal gift.

HEIDI: I'll send a Mister Coffee. *Extends her hand.* Bye, Scoop. Congratulations.

SCOOP *holds her hand:* I'm sorry I disappointed you.

HEIDI: I don't give grades.

SCOOP: I told you in New Hampshire you'd be the one this would all make such a difference to.

HEIDI: I've yet to torch lingerie.

SCOOP: We're talking life choices.

HEIDI: I haven't made them yet.

SCOOP: Yes, you have, or we'd be getting married today.

HEIDI: Scoop, we'd never break a glass at the Pierre.

SCOOP: I didn't marry Lisa because she's Jewish.

HEIDI: No, you married her because she's blandish.

SCOOP: I never meant to hurt you.

HEIDI, *averting his eyes:* I gotta go or Peter will abandon me for a waiter. He's into waiters.

SCOOP: Really? But he's a well-educated man. He went to Williams.

HEIDI: Williams men like to come home to a well-set table too.

SCOOP: Vicious dumpling.

There is a drumroll and then the voice of the master of ceremonies next door is heard.

MASTER OF CEREMONIES: Ladies and gentlemen, Lisa and Scoop have requested this recording of their favorite song.

"You Send Me" is heard. HEIDI *motions* SCOOP *to the door. He starts to leave.* HEIDI *sits down and begins to cry silently.* SCOOP *reenters the room and they look at each other.*

SCOOP: Are you guarding the chips?

They simultaneously move toward each other and kiss. They are suddenly slow-dancing.

SCOOP *laughs:* The editor of *Hustler?*

They continue to dance as the music plays.

HEIDI: Sam Cooke.

SCOOP: A+ content.

HEIDI: A+ form.

SCOOP: I love you, Heidi. I'll always love you.

HEIDI *shakes her head slightly:* Oh, please . . . *Puts her head
     on his shoulder.*
SCOOP *holds her tightly as he sings:*
               Darling, you send me.
               Honest you do.
               Honest you do.
Lights fade as they slow-dance.

ACT TWO

Prologue

1989. Lecture hall, Columbia University. Slides are projected during the lecture.

HEIDI: Lilla Cabot Perry, 1848 to 1933, was, along with the better-known Mary Cassatt and Berthe Morisot, a major influence in American Impressionism. Her painting "Lady with a Bowl of Violets" . . . *Pauses as wrong slide comes on the screen.* Lilla went through a little-known hostility period. . . . Actually, the painting you're looking at is "Judith Beheading Holofernes" by Artemisia Gentileschi. Please bear with me. My T.A. is taking the law boards today.

The correct slide comes on. Thank you. "Lady with a Bowl of Violets." Notice how the tones move from cool blues and violets to warmer oranges lighting up the collar of the rather flimsy negligee. Change flimsy to flouncy. But Lilla cops out when she gets to the head. Suddenly, we're back to traditional portraiture, with the lines completely delineated.

The painting I prefer is "Lady in Evening Dress," painted in 1911. Closer to her mentor Monet; Lilla here is willing to lose her edges in favor of paint and light. Go, Lilla! Now let's compare for a moment Cabot's "Lady" with Lily Martin Spencer's fading rose. There is something uniquely female about these paintings. And I'm not referring to their lovely qualities, delicate techniques, or overall charm. Oh, please! What strikes me is that both ladies seem slightly removed from the occasions at hand. They appear to watch closely and ease the way for the others to join in. I suppose it's really not unlike being an art historian. In other words, being neither the painter nor the casual observer, but a highly informed spectator.

Scene 1

1980. SCOOP *and Lisa's apartment. A pile of opened boxes and wrapping paper are on the coffee table.* LISA *is very pregnant;* BETSY, *around 35, is also pregnant;* DENISE, *24, wears a suit, tie, and sneakers; and* SUSAN *has a new look, with pants, heels, and silk blouse.* BETSY *is making a hat out of wrapping paper. "Imagine" is playing in the background.* LISA *pulls a tiny robe, tiny gown, and tiny slippers from a gift box.*

LISA, *holding up the gown:* Ooooooooh, that's adorable!
DENISE: It's a robe and a nighty. Lisa, that's the cutest thing I've ever seen.
SUSAN: Look at those tiny slippers. How could anything be so tiny?
BETSY: Shhhh! Let's listen to this.

They listen, for a moment, to Lennon singing "Imagine."

SUSAN: I don't think I can listen to much more of this or I'll start crying. *Takes the record off.*

LISA: Denise, let's put on a different song. Something snappy from when they were all together. Like "Rocky Raccoon."

SUSAN: "It's Been a Hard Day's Night" was on my stereo the first time I slept with my high-school/first-year-of-college boyfriend. His signature was twisting and smoking simultaneously.

LISA: "Here Comes the Sun" was on my stereo the first time I slept with Scoop.

BETSY: Really!

LISA: What can I say? I've always been an oddly well-adjusted and cheerful person.

DENISE: You're just normal.

LISA: Thank you, Denise. You're a sweet sister.

Doorbell rings.

SUSAN: That must be Heidi.

LISA: Cha-cha will get it.

SUSAN: I told Heidi to come right over after the park.

BETSY: I can't believe people actually went to that.

SUSAN: She was curious. And I think she was really upset.

BETSY: Well, we were all upset! But the thought of mass weeping with Yoko in Central Park . . .

HEIDI: Hi. Hi. Sorry I'm late. Lisa, lovely to see you again.

SUSAN: See, you can tell she's been living in England. She says "lovely" every chance she gets. Heidi, this is Lisa's sister, Denise. And you know Betsy.

BETSY *shakes Heidi's hand:* Sure. We go back to my *Liberated Earth News* days.

HEIDI: Oh, Betsy, hi.

LISA: Betsy's now managing editor of Scoop's magazine.

HEIDI: I saw a copy of *Boomer* in London. Looks terrific.

BETSY: Lisa, let's get this woman some wine.

LISA *gives* HEIDI *some wine and offers more to* SUSAN: Susie, how 'bout some more.

SUSAN: I can't. I've been living on rabbit food for a month now and I'm still a truck.

LISA: Scoop says that you're the most handsome woman he knows.

SUSAN: Handsome means truck.

BETSY: My sweet husband says men prefer a woman with a little thigh.

SUSAN: Well, all right. Lisa, open another gift!

BETSY: Definitely time for another gift.

DENISE *hands* LISA *another present.*

LISA: Denise, who was that nighty from?

DENISE *looks at a list she's been keeping:* Patti Bennett.

LISA: Why did Patti leave so early?

BETSY: Patti's daughter didn't get into kindergarten at Ethical Culture, and now Charlie's making the entire family go into therapy.

HEIDI: You're joking.

BETSY: Today's their first session.

HEIDI: Really?

BETSY *pats her stomach:* Sure. I've already signed this one up for a cram course for the ERBs.

HEIDI: What's that?

BETSY: They're the SATs for nursery school.

HEIDI: And they have cram courses? I really have been living out of the country for too long.

LISA: What's Charlie Bennett's daughter's name?

SUSAN: Jennifer.

LISA: Oh, I hate those J names. So common. Scoop wants to call this one Maggie, or Pierre in honor of his French-Canadian roots. *Looks at a card.* This is from Susie!

SUSAN: This one's a thank-you present. With Heidi gone, I couldn't have survived moving here without you and Scoop.

DENISE: Where did you live before?

SUSAN: Montana.

DENISE: You lived in Montana?

SUSAN: Before business school I belonged to a Women's Health and Legal Collective there.

DENISE: You mean like a dude ranch?

SUSAN: Like a feminist dude ranch.

HEIDI: Denise, have you never heard of a women's collective?

DENISE: Oh, sure I have. I took women's studies at Brown. LISA *pulls a leopard Snugli out of the box.* Oh, this is fabulous!

LISA: I've never seen a leopard Snugli!

BETSY: That's hysterical!

DENISE: I love it! Don't you love it, Heidi? Susan, this gift could only have come from you. I mean, it's just so Susan!

SUSAN: That's me! Wild, practical, and fifty-percent rayon.

LISA: Thank you. Susie, what did you decide to do about L.A.?

DENISE: Yeah?

SUSAN: I've accepted the position.

BETSY: What position?

SUSAN: I just took a job in L.A. as executive VP for a new production company. They wanted someone with a feminist and business background. Targeting films for the twenty-five-to-twenty-nine-year-old female audience.

BETSY: Lisa, you know some fantastic women. I tell you, this is one power shower! *Toasts.*

DENISE, *toasting:* Hear! Hear!

SUSAN: Heidi, I know some of those Hollywood people can be pretty dreadful, but if I don't do it, someone who cares a lot less will.

DENISE: I'd move to L.A. in a minute. *Picks up the last box.* This one has no card.

HEIDI: Oh, oh that's mine!

LISA: Heidi, Scoop was so excited when I told him Susie invited you here today. He's really sorry to have missed you. He had to go to Princeton for one of those "looking forward to the eighties, looking back on the seventies" panels.

BETSY: I should have been on that panel. I smoked and drank things with Scoop on the *Liberated Earth News* in 1969 that could make Three Mile Island look like a health spa.

SUSAN: The topic was something like "What does the election of Ronald Reagan mean to the greening of America?"

HEIDI: Good question.

DENISE: Well, everyone says he's the best for the economy. Cheer up, kids. The eighties are going to be great.

SUSAN *notices* HEIDI *looking away:* Heidi, are you okay?

HEIDI: Oh, I'm fine. I just had to get up early to meet Peter at the park.

LISA: Heidi, you should grab him. Maybe he'll change. He obviously loves children.

BETSY: Who's this?

LISA: Peter Patrone. Betsy, you know him. *Boomer* did that cover story on him.

BETSY: Oh, "The Best Pediatrician in New York under Forty."

DENISE: Is he married?

HEIDI: Well, actually, he finally broke up last month with Stanley.

DENISE: Oh, fuck piss!

LISA: Denise!

DENISE: I'm sorry, but there's absolutely no one. And once my career's in place, I definitely want to have my children before I'm thirty. I mean, isn't that what you guys fought for? So we could "have it all." I mean, don't you want to have a family, Heidi?

HEIDI: Yes. I hope so.

LISA: You have plenty of time, Heidi.

SUSAN: Well, you almost got married in England.

BETSY: But what happened?

HEIDI: I got this job at Columbia, and he wanted to stay in London.

BETSY: Oh, it's just so unfair. All my single women friends are just such fabulous attractive people! I wish I knew someone for each of you. But Denise is right. There's absolutely no one.

LISA *opens the box and pulls out a furry, funny stuffed animal:* Heidi, this is *so* sweet!

BETSY: Look at its little head.

SUSAN *grabs it:* I want to marry this.

DENISE: I can't believe it. I mean this could only have come from you.

HEIDI: I know. It's just so "Heidi"! Actually, it's a Heffalump. Half elephant, half Hippo. From a Winnie the Pooh story.

BETSY: I'm a Heffalump. Half elephant, half lump. Well, now that I've drunk enough to deliver through my nasal passage. I have to tell you, Heidi, that I loved *And the Light Floods in from the Left*.

DENISE: You know, a lot of people are talking about your book, Heidi. This TV show I'm like a production assistant at, "Hello, New York," is devoting a series to "Women in the Eighties." What we've gained. What we've lost. And April, she's our host, was very excited when I told

her that I'd be seeing you today. *Phone rings.* We thought
we could do something on you and Women in Art. Excuse
me. *Rushes out of the room.*

LISA: My little sister is so up and positive. I just get so tired
sometimes.

BETSY: I get tired all the time.

HEIDI: Me too.

BETSY: Lisa, why doesn't Denise have a Southern accent?

SUSAN: Maybe she liberated it during women's studies at
Brown.

LISA: My little sister is "The New South."

DENISE *reenters:* Lis, it's your husband. He's still at Princeton.

LISA: Please don't say anything juicy till I get back. *Exits.*

Pause.

BETSY, *quietly:* I honestly don't think she knows.

DENISE: Oh, Lisa knows. She was being really cheerful. That
means she knows.

BETSY: Honestly, you should see his little friend. She's a
graphics assistant on the magazine. And now she runs
around New York in leather miniskirts and fishnet stockings. And she's not very bright. She's like that entire generation. Except for you, Denise. They have opinions on
everything and have done nothing. I'm sorry, Heidi. It's
just someone we don't care for very much.

HEIDI: You mean the woman Scoop's seeing?

SUSAN: What?

HEIDI: Susie, this morning I was with the best pediatrician
under forty at the John Lennon memorial in Central Park,
and Scoop was not at Princeton. Scoop and the graphics
assistant were also in Central Park.

SUSAN: Maybe it wasn't him.

HEIDI: Oh, it was him. He embraced me, shook hands with Peter, and said it was very important we were all there. He said this was for our generation.

BETSY: So you met her?

HEIDI: Yes. Fishnet Stockings has opinions.

SUSAN: Was he mortified?

HEIDI: No. He told me my book was A – inspiration, B follow-through.

SUSAN: That's all?

HEIDI: He apologized. He said he didn't want to be rude, but he was too moved to speak. Then he cried, she cried, and they walked away.

BETSY: Well, I'm certainly touched.

SUSAN: Oh, she's just horrible!

BETSY: Susie, what about *him*?

HEIDI: I wasn't surprised really. I wasn't impressed. But I wasn't surprised.

BETSY: I like men. But they're really not very nice.

LISA *reenters:* Who's not very nice?

DENISE: Oh, this guy who works at *Boomer* that someone was going to fix me up with.

LISA: But who were you huddling about when I came in?

BETSY: You.

LISA: Me?

BETSY: We finished your hat. *Gives* LISA *the hat made from wrapping paper and ribbon, and begins to tie it on her.*

LISA: What? Oh, gosh! I wish you all knew how much I appreciate this. Betsy's right: you are fantastic women. *Begins to cry.* Oh, oh, yuck. I'm sorry. Scoop says I'm like an emotional bumper car.

SUSAN *puts her arm around* LISA: That's okay, honey.

LISA: Honest to God, I love women. I really do. *Gathers herself together.* Okay, end of Lisa's dumb episode. Betsy, let's continue our tribute.

BETSY *puts her arm around* LISA: Lisa! Are you . . . ?

LISA *smiles:* Shake your booties, Betsy. BETSY *goes to put the record back on.*

SUSAN: Wait! First a farewell to John. To John.

The women stand up with wineglasses.

ALL: To John!

HEIDI: And Ringo, and Paul, and George . . .

LISA: Forever!

ALL: And Ringo, and Paul, and George, forever!

They toast as "Imagine" plays and the lights fade. HEIDI *puts her arm on Lisa's.*

Scene 2

1982. A TV studio. A studio attendant is on stage calling light cues.

TV ATTENDANT: Give me 189. Let's restore it.

VOICEOVER: Steve to control room, please. Steve to control room.

SCOOP *and* PETER *enter.*

PETER: Ready for my close-up, Mr. De Mille.

TV attendant puts microphones on SCOOP *and* PETER.

SCOOP: I think it's a terrific idea of Lisa's sister to have us all on the show together. Too bad Susie couldn't make it.

PETER: Who's Susie?

SCOOP: Susan.

PETER: Oh, the radical shepherdess.

SCOOP: Now the studio vice president.

TV ATTENDANT: You're all set.

DENISE, *very pregnant, enters with* HEIDI.

DENISE: Hi, guys.

HEIDI: Hi, Scoop.

SCOOP: Hi, Heidi. Great to see you.

TV ATTENDANT: Where do you want her?

DENISE: In the middle. Thanks for coming. We're all very excited about this segment. You're a real cross section.

SCOOP: Peter, this is Lisa's sister, Denise.

PETER: Oh, hi.

DENISE: Lisa says I have to use you for this one. She says you're the best. *Directs them to their seats.* You're there and you're there.

HEIDI: Congratulations on the new baby.

SCOOP: Number two. Way to go, Rosenbaum.

DENISE: Okay. Okay. *Looks at her clipboard.* Some of the topics April wants to cover today are the sixties, social conscience, relationships, Reaganomics, money, careers, approaching the big 4-0; Scoop: opinions, trends; Heidi: women in art, the death of ERA, your book; Peter: the new medicine, kids today; and April says the further out you can take your sexuality, the better. Our audiences enjoy a little controversy with their coffee.

PETER, *stunned*: What?

VOICE: Ten seconds please.

APRIL *enters; the show theme plays:* Hi, guys.

TV ATTENDANT: Five, four, three . . . *Hand-signals two, one,
    go to* APRIL.

APRIL: If you've just joined us, I'm April Lambert. This is
    "Hello, New York." We're speaking today with members
    of the baby boom generation, the kids who grew up in
    the fifties, protested in the sixties, were the "me's" of the
    seventies, and the parents of the eighties. Here with us
    today are Scoop Rosenbaum, editor of the very successful
    and influential *Boomer* magazine; Heidi Holland, author
    of *And the Light Floods in from the Left* and director of
    Womanzart. Is that pronounced like Mozart?

HEIDI: Well, actually, it's Woman's Art.

APRIL: Excuse me, Woman's Art, a group dedicated to the
    recognition of American women artists. And Dr. Peter
    Patrone, who is, according to *Boomer* magazine, for two
    years now, the leading pediatrician in New York under
    forty. Boy, I'm impressed! Good morning to all of you.

PETER: Good morning, April. First of all, let me say I think
    a standard for success for our generation is being able to
    say "Good morning, April!" in person. I have to say I
    am very grateful for this opportunity, April.

APRIL: Thank you. Scoop, you've been an editor since 1967,
    when you started the *Liberated Earth News.* You've cer-
    tainly had a lot of success since then.

SCOOP: April, I'm just a simple newspaperman.

APRIL: Do you think the values of our generation have
    changed significantly since the sixties?

SCOOP: April, I think we're a generation that is still idealistic,
    and idealists wonder what they're going to do when they
    grow up. I'll be wondering till I'm eighty.

APRIL: I once heard the same thing about Bertrand Russell. Heidi, how do you feel about that?

HEIDI: I don't really know much about Bertrand Russell.

APRIL: Peter, you're a doctor. You work with children. Do you see yourself as a grown-up?

PETER: Yes. I'm very old and very wise.

APRIL: We were known as the baby boom generation. Do you think starting our own families now makes a difference in accepting our place as adults?

SCOOP: April, I have two children, Maggie and Pierre. My wife and I were into Canadians at the time. Whether they make me an official adult or not, I really don't know. But having my own family has certainly pulled me out of any "me" generation residue. The future is about my kids, not me.

APRIL: Lucky kids. Heidi, there's a lot of talk these days about superwomen. Are you a superwoman?

HEIDI: Oh, gosh, no. You have to keep too many lists to be a superwoman.

APRIL: I love lists. You should see my refrigerator.

PETER: Do you keep lists *in* your refrigerator?

APRIL *laughs:* Well, they can't say we don't have a sense of humor. Heidi, a lot of women are beginning to feel you can't have it all. Do you think it's time to compromise?

HEIDI: Well, I think that depends on . . .

SCOOP: Can I interrupt and say that I think if we're asking women to compromise, then we also have to ask men to compromise. This year, my wife, Lisa, won the Widener Prize for her illustrations in *King Ginger Goes to Summer Camp.* I'm every bit as proud of that as I am of *Boomer* magazine.

APRIL: But, Scoop, everyone isn't as capable as Lisa. For

instance, a lot of my single women friends are panicked now about their biological clocks winding down. Do you find that's true, Heidi?

HEIDI: If you look . . .

PETER *cuts her off:* April—can I still call you "April"?

APRIL: You have the sweetest face. Can we get a close-up of this face?

PETER: April, I run one of the largest pediatric units in this country. And I am here to tell you that most women can have healthy and happy children till well after forty-two.

APRIL: Well, my friends will certainly be happy to hear that. *Leans toward Peter.* Peter, so far you've chosen not to have children.

PETER: I think, April, what distinguishes our generation from the previous one is our belief that any individual has a right to pursue his or her particular life-style. In other words, say you want to dress up as a Tylenol capsule to host "Hello, New York" tomorrow . . . *In mock camp:* I'd say there's no need, but why not? Go for it!

APRIL *looks at him and back at her card.*

APRIL, *to* HEIDI: So what's next? After the kids and the country house. Once we're settled, Heidi, do you think we'll see a resurgence of a social conscience?

HEIDI: Well, there's . . .

PETER *cuts her off again:* Yes. Betsy Bloomingdale will be at the barricades.

APRIL: Heidi . . .

SCOOP: There's a line in a Ferlinghetti poem: "And I am awaiting the rebirth of Wonder." I think we're all awaiting a rebirth of wonder.

PETER, *sharply:* What does that mean exactly? I wonder.

APRIL: I'm afraid we have only a minute left. Scoop, *Boomer* magazine was an immediate success. Something very rare in the magazine business. Why?

SCOOP: Well, as you've seen this morning, we're serious people with a sense of humor. We're not young professionals, and we're not old lefties or righties. We're unique. We're powerful, but not bullies. We're rich, but not ostentatious. We're parents, but we're not parental. And I think we had the left magazines in college, we had the music magazines in the seventies, and now we deserve what I call a "power" magazine in the eighties. We're opinion- and trend-setters, and I hope *Boomer* is our chronicle.

APRIL: It certainly looks like it's heading in that direction. *Turns back to the cameras.* The baby boom generation, are they all grown up now? Well, they're rich, powerful, famous, and even parents. But who knows what we'd do if Peter Pan came through our bedroom window. PETER *gasps as he hears this.* Thank you, Scoop Rosenbaum, editor of *Boomer* magazine; Heidi Holland, essayist, curator, feminist; and Dr. Peter Patrone, chief of pediatrics at New York Hospital.

PETER: Thank you, April. Good-bye, New York.

APRIL: Bert will be back with the weather in just a moment.

The theme music comes back on. When it is over, APRIL *immediately gets up.*

APRIL *reenters:* A Tylenol capsule! You're too much.

DENISE *reenters:* April, Senator Moore's wife is here with "Divorced Senate wives modeling coats for spring" in Studio Three. Fabulous segment, guys. *To* PETER. You— the Senate wives loved Betsy Bloomingdale.

APRIL: Denise, would you go get my book?

DENISE *exits.*

APRIL *begins shaking hands:* That was tremendous, guys. Thanks for coming. Sorry I have to rush off, but take your time.

SCOOP: April, Lisa and I are meeting a few people at Le Cirque for lunch later. Why don't you and David join us?

APRIL: Who else will be there?

PETER: Oh, the regulars: Farrah and Ryan, Noam Chomsky, Bishop Tutu, Bernie Bosanquet.

APRIL: Who?

SCOOP: Bernard Bosanquet, nineteenth-century British political philosopher.

APRIL: So he's not coming.

SCOOP: No. Peter's being cynical again.

APRIL: That face is so sweet and that mind is so savage.

PETER: Oh, I like savage. Say that again.

SCOOP: Actually, my friend Paul's in town. Heidi, you met Paul in Manchester years ago.

PETER: Is "Paul" Paul Newman?

APRIL: We'll come.

VOICE: April to Studio Three.

APRIL: Scoop, wait here. I'll be right back. *Exits.*

PETER *declaims:*

> Whan that Aprille with *her* shoures soote
> The droghte of human stupidity
>   hath perced to the roote.

SCOOP *whispers:* April Lambert is irrelevant. David Lambert owns sixty buildings in Manhattan. Peter, you were hilarious. I enjoyed myself immensely.

PETER: Of course you did. You won.

SCOOP: I'd say if anyone won it was Heidi. She didn't feel

compelled to be cynical like you or go out for another A
like me.

PETER: No. She didn't say anything.

HEIDI: How could I say anything when both of you were so
eager and willing to say it for me? You two should become
regulars here. The cynic and the idealist. A real cross
section.

SCOOP: Heidi, honey, calm down.

HEIDI, *quite angry:* You have no right to call me honey, or
tell me to calm down.

SCOOP: It's not my fault you didn't say anything.

HEIDI: Excuse me, I have to meet a painter downtown.

SCOOP: Who?

HEIDI: No one you know. C technique. A+ use of color.

SCOOP: Andrea Rothstein.

HEIDI: How do you know Andrea Rothstein?

SCOOP: You obviously don't read *Boomer* magazine.

HEIDI: No.

SCOOP: Andrea was last week's "Hot Spot."

PETER: I once heard the same thing about Bertrand Russell.

HEIDI: Oh, please, Peter. *Begins to exit.* I have to go.

SCOOP *stops her:* Stay a minute. Heidella, I never see you.
I'd love to talk.

HEIDI: That painter is waiting for me.

SCOOP *puts his arm around her:* Heidella, work just isn't
enough. That's what I've learned.

HEIDI: Scoop, I came here to talk about Women and Art.

SCOOP: You're such a wonderful person. You deserve someone wonderful. Heidi, you're clutching your purse.

HEIDI: I have valuables. I'm very late. *Exits.*

SCOOP *calls after her:* Come to the house and see us. We miss
you. *To* PETER: I didn't mean to upset her. We were once
very close.

PETER: Yup.

SCOOP: You and she are still very close.

PETER: Yup.

SCOOP: That's nice. You know, I'm sorry I never really got to know you. You seem like a very nice man.

PETER: Are you having a sentimental spasm? You seem to be sorry, moved, and touched at the drop of a hat. It's sort of manic.

SCOOP: Fatherhood changes people.

PETER: Oh, please . . .

SCOOP: Heidi says that. "Oh, please." You and Heidi have managed to maintain a friendship. I envy you that. How do you do it?

PETER *gets up:* Scoop, I'd like to leave before April comes back.

SCOOP: Peter, do people like you ever wonder what it's all for?

PETER: People like you run the world. You decide what it's all for.

SCOOP: You know what genuinely surprises me? You're a far more arrogant man than I am.

PETER: Scoop, I'm just a simple man of medicine. And now I leave you to await the rebirth of wonder. *Exits.*

SCOOP *is left seated alone on the "Hello, New York" set. He stares out.*

Scene 3

1984. HEIDI *is sitting at a table in a trendy New York restaurant. She looks around.* SUSAN *enters and waves at other people.*

SUSAN: Sorry I was on the phone so long. But we have four shows shooting. *Waves.* I just know everybody in this restaurant. There must be no one in L.A. Everybody's here. Honey, I'm so glad you called me. It's so nice to see you.

HEIDI: It's nice to see you.

SUSAN: I'm famished. Are you famished? Why hasn't our lunch come yet? The service here is very slow. So where were we? I want to know everything. What did you say you've been doing recently?

HEIDI: I've been working. I got a grant to put together a small show of Lilla Cabot Perry. She was an American painter from the Cabot family who spent ten years living next door to Monet.

SUSAN: Are you writing?

HEIDI: A little. "Women and Art." "Women and Madness." "Women and Bran." The usual.

SUSAN: Jesus, I miss talking to real people. Waiter, where is our lunch? We've been sitting here for at least an hour. So, Heidi, dear. Sex and violence. Are you seeing anyone?

HEIDI: Well, there's this lawyer. He calls me "angel" and says he loves me, but he doesn't like me to call him after ten o'clock.

SUSAN: Oh, I hate curfews.

HEIDI: So, no, there's no one important.

SUSAN: I just broke up with my boyfriend. He's fabulous. He's fifty-six, he's still married, and he doesn't want to start another family. And I at least want to keep my options open. I tell you, Heidi, it's rough. Every other woman I know is either pregnant or just miscarried. Honestly, I've been to more fertility lunches.

HEIDI: I'm planning to start my family at sixty. I hear there's a hormone in Brazil.

SUSAN: Honey, we'll shoot a movie there and take treatments.

HEIDI *takes Susan's hand across the table:* Susie, do you ever feel . . .

SUSAN: Heidi, if we've reached the part of the conversation when I tell you what I did alone for my thirty-fifth birthday, I am frankly not interested.

HEIDI: It's not that. It's just . . .

SUSAN: You know, you've developed this bizarre habit of not finishing sentences. Good thing in your business you don't have to take too many meetings.

HEIDI: Susie, do you ever think that what makes you a person is also what keeps you from being a person?

SUSAN: I'm sorry, honey, but you're too deep for me. By now I've been so many people, I don't know who I am. And I don't care. *Laughs.* Honey, I've been thinking a lot about you and how much I love you, and I promise I have the answer for both of us. I'm just waiting to tell you when Denise gets here.

HEIDI: Denise!

SUSAN: Yes, Lisa's sister, Denise. I hired her as my assistant. She's so quick. She's already a story editor. She's just adorable.

HEIDI: But Susie, I called you because I was hoping we could talk . . .

SUSAN: Honey, of course we're going to talk. No one goes to lunch to eat. Oh, good, there's Denise.

DENISE *comes over to the table, followed by the* WAITER.

SUSAN: So what did you tell him?

DENISE: I said we respect him and his talents, and that's why we bought the property. But we have no creative slot for

him. Period. *Kisses* HEIDI. Hi, Heidi. It's great to see you
again.

HEIDI: You too. Congratulations on your job.

DENISE: Thanks. I'm very lucky. I work for a pretty incredible
lady.

SUSAN: So, you hungry?

DENISE: No. I'll just have coffee.

SUSAN: Waiter, one coffee. And I'll have my swordfish dry.
No butter at all.

WAITER *leaves*.

SUSAN: Heidi, when I told Denise you called me yesterday,
we were both very excited. Besides for the obvious reason
that we love you and miss you and you're one of our
favorite people in the world. These bread sticks are fabulous! For a while now I've been wanting to put together
a half-hour show about three women turning thirty in a
large urban center. It can be New York, Chicago, Houston. There are at least ten other single-women series cur-
rently being developed. But your history with women and
art could make us a little different.

DENISE: They've already done doctors, lawyers, nurses, and
detectives. But when you called, we realized that no one
has touched the art world.

SUSAN: What we're interested in is, say, a way-out painter,
an uptight curator, and a dilettante heiress in a loft.

HEIDI: In Houston?

SUSAN: Wherever. You don't have to write; we'll hire a writer.
It's a package, and we want you as our consultant.

HEIDI: Susie, I'm an art historian and essayist. I'm very flat-
tered, but . . .

SUSAN: Maybe some network executive who actually read a

book five years ago will recognize your name and buy the
pilot.

WAITER *arrives:* Salmon. And the swordfish.

SUSAN *looks at her plate and calls to the* WAITER: I'm sorry.
I see butter on this. I can't eat butter.

WAITER: I told them no butter.

SUSAN: Well, they didn't listen. Don't bring it back. I don't
have any more time. Heidi, you and I are people who
need to commit. I'm not political anymore. I mean, equal
rights is one thing, equal pay is one thing, but blaming
everything on being a woman is just passé.

DENISE: Really.

SUSAN: Okay, three gals on the town in an apartment. Cu-
rators, painters, sculptors, what have you.

DENISE: All we need is three pages. Who these people are.
Why they're funny.

HEIDI: But I have no idea who these people are. Or why
they're funny.

DENISE: They're ambitious, they're professional, and they're
on their way to being successful.

SUSAN: And they don't want to make the same mistakes we
did.

HEIDI: I don't want to make the same mistakes we did. What
exactly were they?

DENISE: Well, like, a lot of women your age are very unhappy.
Unfulfilled, frightened of growing old alone.

HEIDI: It's a good thing we're not doing a sitcom about them.

DENISE: Oh, I know. I can't imagine my life without my
husband or my baby, Max. Our girls have a plan. They
want to get married in their twenties, have their first baby
by thirty, and make a pot of money. It's just a much more
together generations than ours.

SUSAN, *looking out:* Is that Diane Keaton? I think that's Diane

Keaton. Heidi, you'll come to L.A. next week. We'll meet with the network and get going on this. Diane looks terrific! I'd love to get her into a series. But until Meryl does a series, none of them will do a series.

HEIDI: Susie, I can't do it either.

DENISE: Why not?

HEIDI: Because I don't think we made such big mistakes. And I don't want to see three gals on the town who do.

SUSAN: Listen, if you don't like this, let's come up with something else.

DENISE *opens her Filofax:* How 'bout a performance artist married to a Korean grocer and living with his entire family in Queens?

SUSAN *cuts off* DENISE: I don't think so. Honey, all we know is, sitcom is big, art is big, and women are big. Like your friend Lily Perry.

HEIDI: Her name is Lilla and she's not my friend. Her dates are 1848 to 1933.

SUSAN: Always the historian. You know, I miss "The Heidi Chronicles." In L.A., everyone creates their own history. Honey, I would love to work with you. I think we could have a lot of fun. And that's not so terrible.

DENISE: Definitely.

SUSAN: Denise, I think Diane is leaving.

DENISE: Oh. I'll go catch her.

SUSAN: Lunch is on me.

DENISE: Heidi, I hope we didn't offend you.

SUSAN: Heidi's not offended. She just doesn't want to do it.

DENISE *extends her hand:* Good-bye, Heidi.

HEIDI: Good-bye, Denise. I'm sorry I didn't have a creative slot for you.

DENISE *rushes out:* Diane!

SUSAN *kisses* HEIDI: Bye, honey. Don't forget we have a date for hormones in Brazil. Wish me luck. *She waves as she did at the high-school dance.*

HEIDI, *looking after her:* Keep the faith.

Scene 4

1986. The Plaza Hotel. We hear the voice-over of SANDRA ZUCKER-HALL: Good afternoon. I'm Sandra Zucker-Hall, president of the Miss Crain's School East Coast Alumnae Association. The topic for today's luncheon is "Women, Where Are We Going," and we are very pleased to have as our speaker a distinguished alumna, Dr. Heidi Holland.

HEIDI, *very well dressed, stands behind a lectern.* Hello. Hello. I graduated from Miss Crain's in 1965, and I look back on my education in Chicago very fondly. One of the far-reaching habits I developed at Miss Crain's was waiting until the desperation point to complete or, rather, start, my homework. Keeping that noble academic tradition alive, I appear before you today with no formal speech. I have no outline, no pink note cards, no hieroglyphics scribbled on my palm. Nothing.

Well, you might be thinking, this is a women's meeting, so let's give her the benefit of the doubt. After teaching at Columbia yesterday, Miss Holland probably attended a low-impact aerobics class *with* weights, picked up her children from school, took the older one to drawing-with-computers at the Metropolitan, and the younger one to swimming-for-gifted-children. On returning home, she immediately prepared grilled mesquite free-range chicken with balsamic vinegar and sun-dried tomatoes, advised her investment-banker well-rounded husband on future finances for the City Ballet, put the children to bed, recited their favorite Greek myths and sex-education legends, dashed into the library to call the twenty-two-year-old squash player who is passionately in love with her to say that they can only be friends, finished writing ten pages of a new book, took the remains of the mesquite free-range dinner to a church that feeds the homeless, massaged her husband's feet, and relieved any fears that he "might" be getting old by "doing it" in the kitchen, read forty pages of the *Inferno* in Italian, took a deep breath, and put out the light. So after all this, we forgive Miss Holland for not preparing a speech today. She's exemplary and exhausted.

Thank you, but you forgive too easily. And I respect my fellow alumnae enough to know that I should attempt to tell you the truth. Oh, hurry up, Heidi. Okay. Why don't I have a speech for the "Women, Where Are We Going" luncheon? Well, actually, yesterday I did teach at Columbia. We discussed Alexander Pope and his theory of the picturesque. And afterward I did attend an exercise class. I walked into the locker room, to my favorite corner, where I can pull on my basic black leotard in peace. Two ladies, younger than me, in pressed blue jeans, were heatedly debating the reading program at Marymount nursery school, and a woman my mother's age was going on and on about her son at Harvard Law School and his wife, a Brazilian hairdresser, who was by no stretch of the imagination good enough for him. They were joined by Mrs. Green, who has perfect red nails, and confessed to anyone who would listen the hardship of throwing her dinner party on the same night as a benefit at the Met. And in the middle of them was a naked gray-haired woman extolling the virtues of brown rice and women's fiction.

And then two twenty-seven-year-old hotshots came in. How do I know they were hotshots? They were both draped in purple and green leather. And as soon as they entered the locker room, they pulled out their alligator datebooks and began madly to call the office. They seemed to have everything under control. They even brought their own heavier weights.

Now Jeanette, the performance-artist-dancer-actress-aerobics teacher, comes in and completes the locker room. I like Jeanette. I've never talked to her, but I like her. I feel her parents are psychiatrists in the Midwest. Maybe Cedar Rapids. Jeanette takes off her blue jeans and rolls her tights up her legs. I notice the hotshots checking out Jeanette's muscle tone while they are lacing up their Zeus low-impact sneakers, and Mrs. Green stops talking about her dinner party to ask where did they find them. Everywhere she has looked on Madison Avenue is out. And the lady with the son at Harvard joins in and says she saw Zeus sneakers at Lord and Taylor and were they any good. Her daughter-in-law likes them, but she can't be trusted. The mothers with the pressed blue jeans leap to her rescue. Yes, they can assure her, despite the daughter-in-law, unequivocally, absolutely, no doubt about it, Zeus sneakers are the best!

It was at this point that I decided I would slip out and take my place in the back row of the class.

I picked up my overstuffed bag. But as I was just between Mrs. Green's raccoon coat and a purple leather bomber jacket, I tripped on one of the hotshots' goddamn five-pound professional weights, and out of my bag flew a week's worth of change, raspberry gum wrappers, and *Alexander Pope on the Picturesque* right on the naked gray-haired fiction woman's foot.

I began giggling. "Oh." "That's okay." "Excuse me." "I'm sorry." "I'm sorry I don't wear leather pants." "I'm sorry I don't eat brown rice." "I'm sorry I don't want to stand naked and discuss Zeus sneakers." "I'm sorry I don't want you to find out I'm worthless. And superior." I'm embarrassed—no, humiliated—in front of every woman in that room. I'm envying women I don't even know. I'm envying women I don't even like. I'm sure the woman with the son at Harvard is miserable to her daughter-in-law. I'm sure the gray-haired fiction woman is having a bisexual relationship with a female dockworker and driving her husband crazy. I'm sure the hotshots have screwed a lot of thirty-five-year-old women, my classmates even, out of jobs, raises, and husbands. And I'm sure the mothers in the pressed blue jeans think women like me chose the wrong road. "Oh, it's a pity they made such a mistake, that empty generation." Well, I really don't want to be feeling this way about all of them. And I certainly don't want to be feeling this way about "Women, Where Are We Going."

I hear whispers. I hear chairs moving from side to side. Yes, I see. I have one minute left.

The women start filing out of the locker room. Jeanette ties her hair in a ponytail and winks at me. "See you in class, Heidi. Don't forget to take a mat this time."

And I look at her pink and kind face. "I'm sorry, Jeanette, I think I'm too sad to go to class."

"Excuse me?" She smiles and grabs a mat.

And suddenly I stop competing with all of them. Suddenly I'm not even racing. "To tell you the truth, Jeanette, I think I better not exercise today."

"Is there anything I can do?" She puts her arm around me. "Are you not well?"

"No, Jeanette. I'm just not happy. I'm afraid I haven't been happy for some time."

Looks up at the audience. I don't blame the ladies in the locker room for how I feel. I don't blame any of us. We're all concerned, intelligent, good women. *Pauses.* It's just that I feel stranded. And I thought the whole point was that we wouldn't feel stranded. I thought the point was that we were all in this together.

Thank you. *Walks off.*

Scene 5

1987. Children's ward in a New York hospital. On the TV is a late-night Christmas movie, Miracle on 34th Street. *A young doctor,* RAY, *is sitting on a child's chair, smoking. There are toys and stuffed animals on the floor, and faded Christmas decorations.* HEIDI *awkwardly enters the room carrying boxes of records and toys as* RAY *turns off the TV.*

HEIDI: Excuse me. Can you help me? I just have one more box.

RAY *stands up:* What?

HEIDI: I just have one . . .

RAY: I'm sorry, the children's ward is closed to visitors after nine o'clock. Can you come back tomorrow?

HEIDI: Actually, no, I can't. Well, I want to make a donation. So I'd like to, uh, drop this off tonight. Maybe if you could tell Dr. Patrone.

RAY: I'm sorry, he's on the phone.

PETER *enters, quite agitated:* Heidi!

HEIDI: Peter.

PETER, *curtly:* What are you doing here?

HEIDI: This is a men's and women's hospital, and I feel the art here does not reflect the makeup of its constituency. So. So. You tell him.

RAY: She's making a donation.

PETER: At midnight!

HEIDI: I tried to reach you all week to say I was coming. Are you here every night?

PETER: When I'm not at the track.

HEIDI: Peter . . .

PETER: Heidi, you don't burst into a goddamn hospital at midnight because you have boyfriend trouble or some other nonsense! Sorry, Ray.

HEIDI: Sorry, Ray.

RAY: That's okay. *Extends his hand*. Thank you for your generous gifts. Merry Christmas.

HEIDI: Merry Christmas.

RAY *exits*.

HEIDI: He seems very nice.

PETER: You seem completely insane.

HEIDI: I have been trying to reach you.

PETER: Well, I'm here every night. It's a hectic social schedule. Cha-cha lessons at five, cocktails and limbo party at six, dinner under the stars at seven, and free love with safe sex at eight.

HEIDI: I thought you went home to Chicago. I found out you were working through the holidays in some metropolitan-news column.

PETER: It was the *New York Times*. "Science Tuesday." Page C1. What did you think of the picture?

HEIDI: I thought you looked good.

PETER: I thought I looked jowly. Turned out the photographer was an ex very close personal friend of Stanley's. He certainly made sure no one would call me. Not even you.

HEIDI: I called you. I couldn't find you.

PETER: Enough. End of narcissism. What can I do for you?

HEIDI *kisses him:* Merry Christmas.

PETER, *chilly:* Thank you.

HEIDI: You're brimming with holiday cheer.

PETER: Heidi, last night three immune-deficient children in Queens were burned out of their home because an entire neighborhood preferred they not return to school next year. I don't know who the hell wants to get in here at midnight. But I can assure you that I'm not very happy that they can.

HEIDI: I should have called again.

PETER: I'm sorry, Heidi. I'm not feeling very communicative. Unfortunately, things here are for real. Not farina.

HEIDI: I've never heard that: for real, not farina.

PETER: Stanley used it.

HEIDI: How is Stanley?

PETER: Oh, he's fine. What's all this?

HEIDI: Nothing.

PETER: This gets better and better. You came here at midnight, Christmas Eve, with boxes of nothing.

HEIDI: It's boxes of books, records, clothing. One girl's complete collection.

PETER: Thank you. We accept. Winter cleaning before the New Year?

HEIDI, *mumbling:* No. Well, actually, I'm leaving tomorrow.

PETER: Heidi, you're mumbling.

HEIDI: I'm going away tomorrow.

PETER: Chicago. See your parents.

HEIDI: I'm going to Northfield, Minnesota. Where the Jesse James band was stopped.

PETER: Are you planning to rob banks and get caught?

HEIDI: I thought I'd finish my new book in the Midwest. I had an offer to teach at Carleton College there. So I accepted.

PETER, *surprised:* This is sudden.

HEIDI: Well, yes, but . . .

PETER: But why not?

HEIDI: Peter, I came to say good-bye.

PETER: Good-bye.

HEIDI: That's it?

PETER: What do you want me to say?

HEIDI: I don't know. You'll call me?

PETER: I'll call you. Heidi, what do you want me to say? You are a brave and remarkable woman. A proud pioneer. My Antonia driving ever forward through the unknown.

HEIDI, *softly:* Peter, sweetie, what is it?

PETER *moves away:* Nothing. *He begins straightening the room, putting toys away.* So you're going to Northfield, Minnesota, to start again. Good-bye, New York. Good-bye, mistakes. Make new friends. Give donations to the old.

HEIDI: I hate it when you're like this.

PETER: Heidi, you arrived at midnight and promptly announced you're leaving tomorrow. I'm just feeling my way through here.

HEIDI: I thought you would be the one person who would completely understand.

PETER, *quite angry:* Understand what? Looking back at your life and regretting your choices? Deciding your work, your friends, your history are totally expendable?

HEIDI: You have a life here that works for you. I don't.

PETER: Right. So I am expendable too.

HEIDI: Peter, stop it!

PETER, *very distant:* I'm not doing anything. I was going to spend a quiet Christmas here with the Hardy Boys.

HEIDI: The Hardy Boys?

PETER: For our last midnight donation, we received my sister-in-law Paula Patrone's complete childhood collection of Nancy Drew, the Bobbsey Twins, the Hardy Boys, Honey Bunch, and *Heidi*, which I actually perused last night in your honor. *Picks up a book from the floor.* Did you know that the first section is Heidi's year of travel and learning, and the second is Heidi uses what she knows? How will you use what you know, Heidi?

HEIDI: I've been sad for a long time. I don't want to be sad anymore.

PETER: This is hard, Heidi. This is very hard. *Begins going through her boxes.* What have we got here? The Mamas and the Papas, Gerry and the Pacemakers, Sam the Sham and the Pharaohs. *Picks up a record.* "Theodore Bikel Sings Favorite Worksongs from the Fourth International."

HEIDI: Scoop's. From his red-diaper period.

PETER: H. W. Jansen, *A History of Art*; Jakob Rosenberg, *Rembrandt's Life and Work*; *The Secret Life of Salvador Dali*; Alice Elizabeth Chase, *Famous Paintings: An Introduction for Young People*; *Mary Cassatt and Philadelphia*. Thank you. We don't have any of these.

HEIDI *smiles:* I thought not.

PETER: The next time some reporter arrives with a surly photographer, I'll tell them, "Never mind the kid's immune system, ask him about the secret life of Salvador Dali."

HEIDI: I think your starting this unit is remarkable.

PETER: Your friend Susan's production company sent us a

very nice check. Who would have thought three women artists in a Houston loft would capture the national imagination? It's odd what people find comforting.

HEIDI: What, sweetie?

PETER: Nothing. I was thinking about what people find comforting. I'm sorry. Generally, I try to stay fairly chipper.

HEIDI: Honey, you don't have to be chipper around me.

PETER: You know what's as unappealing in its own insidious way as my sarcasm?

HEIDI: What?

PETER: Your trying too hard. The high voice, the gratuitous "honey" or "sweetie." I can't tell what the hell you're thinking! *He throws one of the dolls across the room.*

HEIDI: Peter, where is all this coming from?

PETER: Truth.

HEIDI: It'd be preferable.

PETER: Okay. Heidi, I'd say about once a month now I gather in some church, meeting house, or concert hall with handsome men all my own age, and in the front row is usually a couple my parents' age, the father's in a suit and the mother's tasteful, a pleasant face. And we listen for half an hour to testimonials, memories, amusing anecdotes about a son, a friend, a lover, also handsome, also usually my own age, whom none of us will see again. After the first, the fifth, or the fifteenth of these gatherings, a sadness like yours seems a luxury.

HEIDI: I understand.

PETER: No, you don't. Not really. I left out one other thing. My friend Stanley isn't very well. That was my call when you so adventurously arrived. That's where all this is coming from.

HEIDI: Peter, I . . .

PETER: You see, my world gets narrower and narrower. A

person has only so many close friends. And in our lives, our friends are our families. I'm actually quite hurt you don't understand that. I'm very sorry you don't find that comforting.

HEIDI: There is no one precious to me in the way you are.

PETER: But obviously I can't help you. And you can't help me. So . . .

HEIDI: So . . .

PETER: My best to Jesse James.

Pause.

HEIDI: Peter, we could try.

PETER: Not if you're off to become someone else.

HEIDI: I could become someone else next year. Postpone it. If that's not a little too understanding.

PETER: A little, but I'm listening.

HEIDI: I promise you won't lose this member of your family.

PETER: Who? The sad one or the one I spotted twenty-five years ago at a Miss Crain's School dance?

HEIDI: Split the difference.

Pause.

PETER: However, if you do stay, I have one specific request.

HEIDI: What?

PETER: That you still plan to donate this very fine collection.

HEIDI: All yours.

PETER *begins going through the records again:* Mitch Ryder and the Detroit Wheels. Gary Puckett and the Union Gap. Nelson and the Rocky Fellers. How did we ever become friends?

HEIDI: I'm a sucker for a man of taste and talent.

PETER: You have such distinguished taste in music. I can tell you're very bright. Tell me, since I value your fine opinion, what did you think of Dr. Ray? *He sits on one of the children's chairs and* HEIDI *sits on a tiny chair beside him.*

HEIDI: I told you I liked him.

PETER: Yes. And I like Greg Louganis. But I don't know if a diver is the best choice for me.

HEIDI: Is Dr. Ray a diver?

PETER: No. But he's a man of taste and talent.

HEIDI *picks up two Dixie cups:* It's a lovely evening, don't you think?

PETER: What?

HEIDI: The stars above us. The sea below us. Tell me, how long have you been on this cruise?

PETER: Oh, around twenty-five years. I tried to pick out your name. Amanda, Lady Clara, Estelle.

HEIDI *notices he's crying:* It's . . .

PETER: I know. It's Heidi. Your old grandfather told me. Are you from the Alps?

HEIDI: Yes. Like chocolate. I want to know you all my life. If we can't marry, let's be great friends.

PETER: I will keep this goblet as a memento beside my pillow. *He looks at her. She takes his hand and gets him up.*

HEIDI: Ah, "The Shoop Shoop Song." Baroque but fragile.

PETER: I'm not familiar with the work.

HEIDI *begins to sing very softly to him:*
      Is it in her eyes?

PETER, *softly, after a moment:*
      Oh, no, you'll be deceived.

HEIDI:
      If you want to know if she loves you so . . .

PETER *embraces* HEIDI.

PETER: Merry Christmas, Heidi.
HEIDI: Merry Christmas, Peter.

Scene 6

1989. Empty room with fireplace, freshly painted white. Warm afternoon sunlight streams in from the left through the window. HEIDI, *seated in a rocker, is reading through a book galley.* SCOOP *enters, dressed for a business lunch in a suit and raincoat.*

SCOOP, *loudly:* Hello. Hello.
HEIDI: Scoop!
SCOOP: Hello. I'm canvassing for Eugene McCarthy for president. Miss Holland, you might be interested in my publication, the *Liberated Earth News*. We tell the truth. The way the people see it. So what's up? This is a nice apartment. What do they call it? Raw space with rocker?
HEIDI: I moved in last week. Furniture hasn't come yet.
SCOOP: You know what you could use here? Chintz. Chintz curtains would be very nice. But not shiny. Be specific.
HEIDI: What do you know about chintz?
SCOOP: Now that's sexist. That's really sexist. I've decorated at least four houses, and I've edited a magazine for ten years that was responsible for the chintz renaissance as we know it today. In fact, do you know why warm Mediterranean colors have returned to the home palette?
HEIDI: Because *Boomer* magazine warned us against the disastrous side effects of too many pastels. Scoop, what are you doing here?
SCOOP: Maritime art.
HEIDI: You came to my raw space for maritime art?

SCOOP: I have an offer to buy maritime art. April Lambert's husband is into equestrian art. So horses are out of the question for me. But I'm considering maritime art. I've always liked Turner.

HEIDI: Well, you can't go wrong with a Turner.

SCOOP: Or a Winslow Homer. So, are you happy?

HEIDI: What?

SCOOP: I made a list the other day of the people I care about. And you made the top ten. In fact, I reworked the list a few times, and you were the only one who made the top ten through three decades. Yup. You and Smokey Robinson were the standards. So if I can keep you on my list, you can tell me if you're happy and why. *Helps himself to a cookie.* Mmmm. Good cookies.

HEIDI: A+ pecan. B− sandy.

SCOOP: Better. B+ sandy.

HEIDI: Actually, I am seeing an editor I seem to like.

SCOOP: Good. Time for my life now. See, I've grown over the years. We did you first. I think that shows remarkable control and sensitivity. Can you keep a secret?

HEIDI: If this involves someone in fishnets twenty-five or younger, not really.

SCOOP: I hate it when you're prissy. Does your editor know you're prissy?

HEIDI: Yes. He's even more prissy than I am. Scoop, why are you here?

SCOOP: Touch base. There aren't that many people in my life who really know me. I sold *Boomer* magazine two hours ago. You're the first to know.

HEIDI: What? Why?

SCOOP: I was at lunch at Lutèce with the potential buyer and his lawyer, and I made a deal with myself. If I could get the lemon soufflé without ordering a day in advance, I'd sell. Have you ever ordered soufflé in advance at Lutèce?

HEIDI: No.

SCOOP: Do it.

HEIDI: I don't want to.

SCOOP: Pick up the phone and do it!

HEIDI: Scoop, stop it.

SCOOP: This is the best dessert I've ever had. *Dials.* Hi, it's Scoop Rosenbaum. I'd like to order two soufflés for tonight.

HEIDI: Scoop, I'm not going to Lutèce for dinner tonight. And I'm certainly not dropping in for dessert. I'm busy.

SCOOP: We're undecided lemon or chocolate. I'll call back.

HEIDI: I have a date.

SCOOP: With whom? That editorial drone next door? Where did he go to school? You're not missing a lemon soufflé at Lutèce for an intimate evening dangling participles. *Dials again.* Hello. This is Mr. Rosenbaum. Who is this? Ah, *bonjour*, Philippe. *Comment allez-vous?*

HEIDI: Scoop, where's Lisa?

SCOOP: She's in Florida with Maggie and her mother. Pierre's in town with me.

HEIDI: Maybe we should call Lisa.

SCOOP: No, we shouldn't call Lisa. *On the phone:* Philippe, *deux citron soufflés.*

HEIDI: All right. Maybe we should call someone else?

SCOOP: You mean, is there a fishnet somewhere in town so you don't have to deal with me tonight?

HEIDI: Something like that. Yes.

SCOOP: No such luck. Philippe, *je, je . . . merci. Hangs up and begins to sing:*

> Baby, I'm yours.
> And I'll be yours
> until two and two are three.

HEIDI: Did you really sell your magazine?

SCOOP: Yup.

HEIDI: Why?

SCOOP: Because I wanted to buy maritime art. Do you know how much they paid me?

HEIDI: No.

SCOOP: I think this raw space could do with a Turner or two. I'll get you a few for Christmas.

HEIDI: But why did you do it?

SCOOP: What's it all for, Heidella? What's it all for?

HEIDI: You liked it.

SCOOP: Yup.

HEIDI: You were good at it.

SCOOP: Yup. And I stopped pastels in the nick of time. And I helped get a few people elected, and a few people investigated. And a single man who likes oral sex when he reads the Talmud placed an ad and married a woman who doesn't. I did all that. Now what?

HEIDI: What do you mean?

SCOOP: Now what? What do I show my children and say, "See, kids, Daddy did that"? Do I say, "See that restaurant, Maggie? Daddy started going there and suddenly everybody was going there until they started going somewhere else"? Do I say, "Pierre, your father was known as an arbiter of good taste in a decade defined as sexy, greedy"? Or is my greatest legacy to them buying a farm in Litchfield County before the land values went soaring. Will my kids say, "My dad was basically a lazy man and a philanderer, but he had a nose for Connecticut real estate, and we love him because he didn't make us weekend in the Hamptons"?

HEIDI: I didn't know you worried so much about your children.

SCOOP: I'm sorry. I mean, we hardly know each other anymore. I'm sorry. *Looks at her.* I'm being very self-
indulgent. Yes?

HEIDI: Yes.

SCOOP: I'm a spoiled man with superficial values. Yes?

HEIDI: Don't look at me like that.

SCOOP: Like what?

HEIDI: Don't look at me with those doe eyes and tell me how
spoiled you are. Next thing I know, you'll tell me you
never meant to hurt me.

SCOOP: Maybe we should try again.

HEIDI: Why?

SCOOP: You're lonely and I'm lost.

HEIDI: Oh, please.

Pause. They both laugh.

SCOOP *smiles:* I thought you might enjoy that.

HEIDI: I did. A lot.

SCOOP: How much?

HEIDI *smiles:* A lot.

SCOOP: So, as my old friend and longtime observer, what do
you think I should do now?

HEIDI: I'd say hold on to the land in Litchfield County.

SCOOP *kisses* HEIDI *on the cheek, she touches his face:* It's
nice to see you, Heidella.

HEIDI: It's nice to see you. *Pats his arm as a friend.* I have
absolutely no idea why Lisa stays married to you.

SCOOP: You would have married me.

HEIDI: But I wouldn't have stayed married to you.

SCOOP: Good thing I'm married to Lisa.

HEIDI: Yup. Good thing.

SCOOP: I never liked your caustic side. You and Peter share that. *Sits on the floor beside her rocker.* How is Peter?

HEIDI: Peter moved in with a nice anesthesiologist named Ray. He still runs that ward, and on weekends they garden at their home in Bucks County.

SCOOP: A handsome doctor and a country house. Peter's living my mother's dream come true! I thought of you both last week when I was flying home from L.A.

HEIDI: You did?

SCOOP: It was nighttime and I recognized Chicago from the sky and I remembered the first time I visited you there. Remember, I spent the day asking for Goethe Street, then I called you and you said "Dummy, it's pronounced "Gothe." Anyway, I wondered if flying over Chicago for my grandchildren would be like driving past an A&W root-beer stand for me. I think about the future all the time now.

HEIDI: Scoop, you didn't sell *Boomer* for a lemon soufflé.

SCOOP: Heidi, on a scale from one to ten, if you aim for six and get six, that's the ball game. So you might as well try for your ten.

HEIDI: If you know what your ten is.

SCOOP: Well, I have a notion. Oh, yes, and one other thing. Susan told me you adopted a baby last week.

HEIDI, *nonchalant:* She did?

SCOOP: Yes. And I thought, "Fuck you. If you have the courage to make the move and go for your ten, then what am I waiting for?"

HEIDI: Wait a minute! Why is my baby my ten, and your work your ten?

SCOOP: I didn't mean it that way.

HEIDI: Well, it certainly came out that way. I am not some empty vessel.

SCOOP: No, you're not. But I appreciate the maritime allusion.

HEIDI: And anyway, I wasn't alone against the wilderness. Peter helped me. Shall I get off my high horse now, or would you like to hear more?

SCOOP: You're cute.

HEIDI: You're deceptive. She's asleep in the other raw space.

SCOOP: This entire time? Why didn't you say anything?

HEIDI: Why didn't you say anything?

SCOOP: What do you call her?

HEIDI: Vicious dumpling.

SCOOP: Really!

HEIDI: Peter suggested Panama Hattie in honor of his favorite musical and her place of birth. I also considered Lilla, Mary, or Grandma, so she'll grow up to be a painter. And Crystal or Ronnette, so she'll grow up to start a girl group. But that's a little . . .

SCOOP: Much. That's a little much.

HEIDI: So I settled on Judy. After "A Date with Judy." She's very pretty. A little cellulite on the toes, but by the time she's twenty, they'll be doing simple nips and toe tucks at Elizabeth Arden.

SCOOP: And are you happy?

HEIDI: I've never been what I'd call a happy girl. Too prissy. Too caustic.

SCOOP: But now. Right now. Are you happy?

HEIDI: Well, I have a daughter. And I've never been particularly maternal. I'm not real practiced at sharing. But, Scoop, there's a chance, just a milli-notion, that Pierre Rosenbaum and Judy Holland will meet on a plane over Chicago. And Pierre will tell her his father named him for a Canadian prime minister, and she'll say she was almost named for someone who sang "My Boyfriend's Back." And he'll never tell her it's either/or, baby. And she'll never think she's worthless unless he lets her have it all. And maybe, just maybe, things will be a little better. And, yes, that does make me happy.

SCOOP: So I was right all along. You were a true believer.

HEIDI: I don't see how it could be any other way.

SCOOP: No regrets.

HEIDI: Just two.

SCOOP: Me?

HEIDI: No. "Hello, New York" and I still never torched lingerie.

SCOOP, *suddenly looking at his watch:* Jesus, *The Wicked Cooks!*

HEIDI: Who?

SCOOP: *The Wicked Cooks.* It's a Günter Grass novel. Pierre's music teacher adapted it for the fourth-grade play at Ethical Culture.

HEIDI: Why don't they do *The Music Man* or *Johnny Appleseed*?

SCOOP: Oh, please. *Pulls out a package from his pocket.* This is for Judy. It's a silver spoon. My secretary picked it out. You can't go wrong.

HEIDI: Hey, Scoop, I think you did the right thing.

SCOOP: Buying the spoon or selling the magazine?

HEIDI: Both. Don't you want to just take a peek at Judy? Stay just a sec. I want her to understand men, and you're a classic. *Leaves the room.*

SCOOP *calls to her:* I'm sort of dating an actress who says I'm withholding. Do you think I'm withholding?

HEIDI: Well, let's just say I don't know who you're saving it for. *Returns with carriage.* Judy Holland, this is Scoop Rosenbaum.

SCOOP: Hi, Judy.

HEIDI: Hi, Scoop.

SCOOP *looks into the carriage:* How ya doing? They all look like Winston Churchill. A+ intelligence, B− vocabulary.

HEIDI: C'mon, be generous. A+ vocabulary.

SCOOP *looks at his watch:* Fuck! The fucking wicked cooks!

HEIDI: Judy, for future reference, Uncle Scoop hates foul language. *Walks him to the entryway.* Bye, Scoop. Thanks for coming to see us.

SCOOP: Hey, Heidella. If I do something crazy, like announce I'm running for Congress next week, will you and Peter be there? Gay Men and Single Mothers for Rosenbaum. Grass-roots movements. A man for all genders.

HEIDI: So that's why you sold your magazine.

SCOOP: All people deserve to fulfill their potential. Judy, that's what your mother told me in 1968 on the first snowy night in Manchester, New Hampshire. America needs heroes.

HEIDI: Scoop, you are many things, but . . .

SCOOP *takes Heidi's hand in a campaign pose:* What do you think, Judy? A mother for the nineties and a hero for the nineties. Bye, Heidella. *Kisses her on the cheek and exits.*

HEIDI *calls after him:* The editor went to Columbia.

SCOOP *calls back:* I knew that!

HEIDI *takes* JUDY *out of the carriage and lifts her up:* A heroine for the twenty-first!

She sits in the rocker and begins to sing softly, adding her own spirited high and low harmonies.

Darling, you send me.

You send me.

Honest you do, honest you do, honest you do.

Lights fade as HEIDI *rocks. The final image of the play, as the audience exits, is a slide of* HEIDI *triumphantly holding Judy in front of a museum banner for a Georgia O'Keefe retrospective.*

END